THE PLEASANT AVENUE CONNECTION

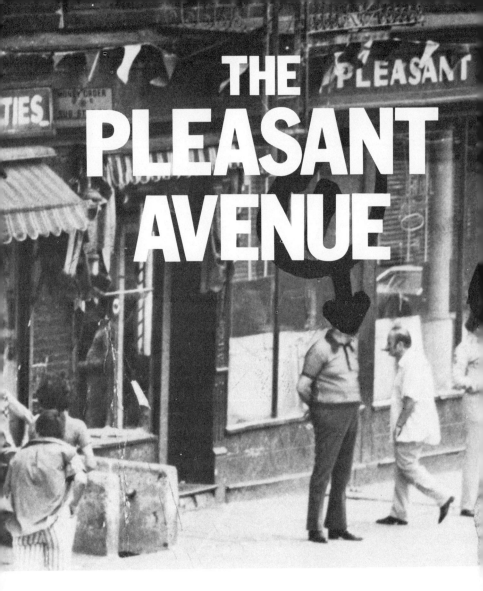

THE PLEASANT AVENUE

David Durk with Arlene Durk

CONNECTION

& Ira Silverman

HARPER & ROW, PUBLISHERS
New York, Hagerstown, San Francisco, London

For the Old Man

In the hope that future promises
will be easier to keep

———

But I have promises to keep,
And miles to go before I sleep,
And miles to go before I sleep.
Robert Frost

FIRST EDITION

Library of Congress Cataloging in Publication Data

Durk, David.
   The pleasant avenue connection.
   1. Narcotics, Control of—New York (City)
2. Heroin. 3. Undercover operations.
I. Silverman, Ira, joint author. II. Durk,
Arlene, joint author. III. Title.
HV5833.N45D87 1976   364.1'57'097471   74–15821
ISBN 0–06–011142–9

76 77 78 79 10 9 8 7 6 5 4 3 2 1

Contents

Acknowledgments, *David Durk*

To those who were part of this story, whose presence in or connection with the criminal justice system has made a meaningful difference in the viability of that system, to past and present members of the New York City Police Department: Deputy Chief Paul Delise, Assistant Chief Arthur Grubert, Deputy Inspector Harold Hess, Detectives Robert Leuci and Bill Irwin, Inspector Patrick Murphy, and two civilians, David Burnham and Henry Ruth.

And to some very special people who were always there: Lieutenant Ronald Reis (NYPD), Special Agent of the FBI Robert Levinson, and A. Tappan Wilder.

To Dr. Irving Durk, my father, and to the old man, both of whom died just before this book came to life and both of whom, in very different ways, influenced my life—my father, who gave me a set of principles, and the old man who provided me with the test of those principles which led ultimately to what this book is all about.

To a first-rate editor and friend, Virginia Hilu, who combined skill and judgment with unflagging enthusiasm, and to Harriet Stanton, who made the pieces fit.

Finally, to the superb men and women, now scattered, who comprised a new type of SIU that I was privileged to command at the direction of former First Deputy Police Commissioner William P. McCarthy, from September 18, 1972, to May 8, 1975: Sergeant Edward P. Powers, Detectives Joseph Flynn, Nicholas Kuzon, Gianpaolo Spinelli, Oswald Markoe, Michael Sullivan, Jerry Aruta, and Henry Cinotti, Police Officer Joanne Meyers, and to Herman Goldfarb, to whom promises were made that I am still trying to keep.

D. D.

Prologue

This is a true story.

It is a story of a small industry run in New York City by very careful men. It is a cottage industry operating out of tenement apartments and storefronts, but it is big enough to process and sell most of the pure heroin available in this country.

It is the story of men in their forties and fifties who started the wholesale heroin business and of younger men in their teens and twenties who run it.

It is also the story of the attempts of a detective to get the New York City Police Department and Mayor Lindsay's administration to take action against the men who actually run the heroin business, not just the street pushers.

And, finally, it is the story of a father's efforts to keep his son out of the heroin business and how these efforts led to Operation Uncover—the largest and probably most important organized crime investigation ever conducted in this country.

Some of the descriptions of actual events and people have been changed to safeguard those still in danger and to protect confidential sources of information.

Sadly, what happened in New York City in the late 1960s and early 1970s—all that is described in these pages—is beginning to happen again in New York, and is happening in towns and cities across this country. There is no business as profitable as the heroin business, and these profits are measured in the lives of our children.

1. The Old Man's Son

In East Harlem, it's called moving a package. A kid with good connections might get to move his first package at sixteen or seventeen. If he does well, he can get to move more and more packages and, within a year, he can begin to earn as much as two or three thousand dollars a week.

The packages might be small: brown paper bags, children's toys, or Crackerjack boxes. Or they might be larger: suitcases, garment bags, or automobile tires. But, in East Harlem, "packages" contain one thing: heroin.

A kid moving a heroin package may take it just two blocks, from one car trunk to another. Or, he may take it to a bus terminal or an airport or, perhaps, to another city—Toledo, Detroit, Atlanta, or St. Louis.

In the argot of the trade, a package is any sizable shipment of heroin, generally a pound or more. In major transactions, the drug is sold by the kilogram, or kilo, a metric weight of a little over two pounds. In recent years, a kilo of pure heroin has sold in the United States for about thirty thousand dollars. Mixed with milk sugar in a recipe of one part heroin to six or seven parts milk sugar, and repackaged in small amounts for sale on the street to addicts, a kilo is worth about five hundred thousand dollars.

The men who run the East Harlem heroin business never move their own packages. To get caught with a package by the police (or by rival dealers) could mean trouble, the kind of trouble that sometimes can't be "fixed up," so the men who run the business lay off the risk of moving packages to neighborhood kids. The kids get paid well and, of equal importance to them, they get the chance of attracting the attention and favor of the most powerful men they have ever heard of—heroin bosses like Herbie Sperling, Gennaro Zanfardino, Johnny Capra, and Gigi Inglese.

In 1969, I knew nothing about kids in East Harlem moving thirty-thousand-dollar heroin packages through the streets in brown paper bags and Crackerjack boxes. After six years in the New York City Police Department, I knew little about narcotics. I was a detective, but I wasn't assigned to the department's Narcotics Division, and I had never worked on a major narcotics investigation.

My introduction to the inner workings of the narcotics business began on a Friday afternoon in January, 1969. Working on an investigation that had nothing to do with narcotics, I met an old man who was from East Harlem and feared his son would soon be moving heroin packages.

The old man worked as a printer in a newspaper plant. He began telling me about his son and about himself as he worked behind a row of Linotype machines. The old man was unpacking foot-long ingots of lead to be melted down and cast into type.

All his life he had lived in East Harlem, and, as a young man, he had been a numbers operator and a loan shark. He said he wasn't accustomed to talking "straight" with policemen, but he was talking to me because he thought I was an honest cop and because he wanted to keep his son out of the heroin business.

"I'm not a saint, David," the old man said. "I've done policy, a little shylocking. Who doesn't want money? But not heroin, not needles in kids' arms.

"My kid, my Vinnie, is smart," the old man said. "Benjamin Franklin High School? I know it stinks. He knows it stinks. He's in the streets more than he's in school. So, I tell him to transfer out. I tell him, Vinnie, go to printing trades school. I tell him to be a printer like me.

"And you know what he tells me? He tells me printing is shit. He says, 'Pop, you know what happened to the *Mirror?* You know what happened to the *Journal-American?* Well, that's what's going to happen to your paper, too. You'll be out on your ass. And then you know where you're going to be? In the bakery with Aunt Sophie making cannoli. And Pop, I'm not a printer. I'm not a cannoli maker. That's shit. I want to be somebody, Pop. You think I want to hang around 112th Street all my life? So leave me alone.' That's what I hear from him—'Leave me alone, leave me alone.' I should close my eyes and leave him alone."

The old man put his hand on my shoulder. "My Vinnie is seventeen years old, and all he knows to tell me is that printing is shit. Okay. Printing is shit. So what does he want to do? In another year he could graduate school. No. Instead he wants to be like his friend, Ernie Boy, and go to work for Nunzi. Nunzi will give him the heroin, and my Vinnie will take it to the niggers, the Cubans. He'll go to the Bronx, to Jersey. Wherever the bread for heroin is, that's where he'll go."

The old man took out his wallet and showed me his son's confirmation picture.

"This is my Vinnie. Good-looking kid, David, right? But he's not thinking. All he's thinking is cars and broads. Broads like the ones that hang around with Nunzi and Capra and Ernie Boy. My kid isn't thinking with his head anymore. Nunzi has got him thinking with his prick. That's what Nunzi has got my kid doing . . . and not only my kid, lots of kids."

The old man wanted me to lock up Ernie Boy. The old man thought that if Ernie Boy got arrested with a package, his son would change his mind about going to work for Nunzi.

"All my kid talks about is Ernie Boy and his new car, Ernie Boy and the broads he's got. I don't want to hear anymore about Ernie Boy. All I want is you should get him good with the stuff and he should sit in Rikers for a fucking year and wear out his pants."

I told the old man that I just couldn't grab Ernie Boy on the street and hope to find heroin on him. I said I would need to know a lot more about Ernie Boy before I could hope to arrest him.

The old man said he was sure he could give me all the information I needed.

"He's got a club up on First Avenue. A social club. The Regency. That's where his action is. I'll take you up there. I'll show you the club. I'll show you everything. I'll show you how the junk moves out of there."

I asked the old man when we could get started.

"I've got to work until eight o'clock. Then I'm off. I could call Evelina and tell her I'll be late. If you could pick me up here, I'll take a ride with you. I'll take you uptown, and you'll see everything."

Shortly before eight o'clock, I parked outside the newspaper plant and waited for the old man. He came out of the building with three or four other men and stopped to talk with them on the sidewalk.

At one point, he turned in my direction and nodded. It was a nod I knew well. He knew I was there, and he wanted me to wait in the car. He would come to me.

When the other men left, the old man stayed in front of the building for a few moments. He put on his gloves, zipped up his stormcoat, and adjusted the brim of his hat. Then he walked to the car and got in the back seat.

"This car is going to heat up real quick, David."

"What do you mean?"

"They're going to make this car. They're going to have no trouble making this car."

I was driving a green Ford. It wasn't a department car. But, the old man said, it looked like one.

"This car says cop all over it. Anybody in the neighborhood sees me in this car, I've got trouble. The only thing we can do is when we get uptown I'll lay on the floor. But they're going to make you. This car will heat up the second time we drive up First Avenue. Believe me, we go twice around the same block, and they'll know you're there."

We began driving uptown, and the old man told me that in the Italian section of East Harlem there are lookouts on almost every block.

"The numbers guys have people watching. The bookmakers have people watching. And Nunzi and guys in junk have got half the neighborhood working for them."

The old man muttered something in Italian and said, "David, somebody's got to get the junk out of East Harlem. Heroin is fucking up everything. Everybody has gone crazy with it. Heroin, heroin, all you see is heroin.

"And our own kids are dying from the stuff, and still we're putting it out on the street. This kid, Fonzo, a friend of my Vinnie. I know him since he was shitting in his diapers. I used to see him on the avenue going to school in the morning, and I'd kick him in the ass. And he'd go running down the street yelling and laughing. That's how well I knew this kid, David. And they give him a hot needle, and he dies from an overdose.

"And you think that makes any difference to the other fucking kids? Nothing. As soon as they hear that Fonzo OD'd everybody's running around wanting to know where he was buying his stuff. The stuff must be dynamite. You understand me, David, the kid dies from it, and all the others are dying to get it because it must be strong stuff. What kind of kids are we bringing up?"

I interrupted the old man. "Where on First Avenue is Ernie Boy's place?"

"The number is 2272. Let's see . . . I think the best way for us is to shoot up the East River Drive to Ninety-sixth Street. Then we'll go over to First Avenue. Nobody knows me until about 112th Street. Then I'll lay on the floor, and we'll go up four or five blocks. There will be Ernie Boy's club and you'll see everything."

As soon as we got off the drive at Ninety-sixth Street, the old man began to watch the streets carefully.

"I think I should lay on the floor right here. We got to pass the hospital, and what if Ernie Boy's mother is walking in for her thyroid pills. She sees me with you, it would be just like if Ernie Boy saw us."

I turned right on First Avenue, heading uptown with the old man stretched out on the floorboard.

We stopped for a light, and the old man asked me where we were.

"At 106th Street," I said.

"Just keep going up the avenue. Ten more blocks and then start watching for the numbers. You're looking for 2272. You can't miss it; there will be lots of cars parked outside. Caddies, Lincolns, Thunderbirds, everything. When you get there, don't stop. Look around, but don't stop. First we'll ride by and check it out and see what's doing."

On 116th Street I caught a red light.

"We got a break," I told the old man. "We're on 116th Street, and the light just turned red."

"Good. It's a long light," the old man said. "Do you see the coffee shop on the corner?"

"Yeah."

"That's the Delightful. That's Buckalo's place. Half the avenue hangs out in there. Heavy action, very heavy. Do you see that luncheonette?"

"Which one?"

"That one." The old man pointed it out. "That's Nunzi's place."

"What do you mean?"

"That's his place, he owns it. It's a regular luncheonette, and he runs his junk business in there."

The light changed to green. "Okay, we're going to move across 116th."

"What do you see, David? What do you see?"

"Not much. Not too many people in the street. Nobody looks like he's doing business. But, there's cars double-parked all over the place. Don't the precinct cops up here give out parking tickets?"

"Parking tickets?"

The old man laughed. "I know for sure you never worked East Harlem. There's no parking tickets up here. The cops are all taken care of. They don't come around here with tickets, and we got some real bad cops up here, David.

"There's one cop that's in the Delightful all the time. He's in there selling guns to the kids moving packages. I know him. He's . . ."

"What! You're telling me that there's a cop up here selling guns?"

"Yeah. What's the big deal? You never heard of a cop selling guns? I'll tell you all about him. But, watch the street. You must be getting close to Ernie Boy's place. Are you looking for the numbers?"

"I don't see it yet. Wait a minute. It's the storefront near the bakery?"

"Right. My dopey Vinnie is probably in there with that fucking Ernie Boy right now. Is the door open? Can you see in?"

"I think the door was closed. We've passed it now. It was very hard to see. There was a goddamned Con Ed truck right in front of it. The Con Ed truck was double-parked. And there was some yo-yo triple-parked next to him. These guys triple-park and don't get tickets? Or towed? Un-fucking-believable."

"They park where they want. They're all over the street. Especially if they're picking up packages, they'll put the car any place. Take it a little slow. I'm gonna try to take a peek out the back window."

"Do you see anything?"

"Yeah. Yeah."

"What do you see?"

"You seen the bronze Lincoln?"

"I'm not sure."

"That's Funzi's car. He picks up for Sally. I didn't see Sal's car, but if Funzi is here, Sal is around. And the car next to the Con Ed truck, the maroon Fleetwood, that belongs to a bakery that delivers up here. There's Ricans or Cubans running the bakery, and they move a lot of stuff. But I think they're doing coke, not junk."

"Do you want me to keep going straight up First?"

"No, no. Make a right when you can. I'll take you over to Pleasant. That's where I live and that's where you have the real heavy action. I'm not talking about shitheels like Ernie Boy. I'm talking about Jerry Z. I'm talking about The Hook. I'm talking about Armando himself."

"Pleasant Avenue is where you got the numbers banks and all the bookies. It's KG action. Right?" (KG's were known gamblers.)

"Numbers and books, that's right. I did numbers twenty years ago right in front of my house. I was working with Whitey Marsh's cousin, and we were controlling all the action from here to Jersey. I was making five, six big ones a week. You know what kind of money that was then? That was good money. But, now the numbers guys can't find room to stand on the sidewalk on Pleasant. It's all junk. Heroin. Everything above 116th Street is junk. And guys I knew for years ain't doing numbers no more. That ain't worth their time anymore. They are all doing junk. Can you imagine? These are guys with their own kids home, and they're putting needles in other kids' arms."

"Where do you want me to go when we get to Pleasant? I'm getting close to the corner."

"Make a right. Take it slow. But not too slow. And the important thing to see is just before you come to 117th Street. On your left there will be a luncheonette and then there will be a barber shop, and right on the corner there'll be a bar. That's the Pleasant Tavern. That's where Jerry Z. is every afternoon. In the morning Louie Fats does numbers in there. And then, in the afternoon, Jerry Z. comes there. Every day. And when Jerry Z. is there, Johnny Echoes is there, that's Ernie Boy's brother-in-law, and Funzi of 111th Street is there, and Funzi of 118th Street is there."

"Which Funzi did you say picks up for Sal?"

"Huh?"

"On First Avenue you told me there's a Funzi that picks up for Sal."

"Oh, that's a different Funzi."

"There's a Funzi of 111th Street, and there's a Funzi of 118th Street, and there's another Funzi?"

"Sure. The Funzi on First Avenue is Bath Beach Funzi. Bath Beach Funzi, David. Bath Beach Funzi picks up for Sal."

My head was swirling with Funzis.

"You never heard of Bath Beach Funzi, David. He's a big mover and shylock. Use to be an ice man. You know, a jewelry fence. Who doesn't know Bath Beach Funzi? The guy's got to have a four-page yellow sheet. How many years you been a cop, David? Tell me the truth, have you ever worked big guys? Or, you been running around picking up winos for spitting on the sidewalk?"

I drove through the "heavy action" blocks of Pleasant Avenue, First Avenue, and 116th Street several times until the old man decided we were drawing too much attention.

"It's getting late. Evelina's going to be worried about me. If you want to talk for a few minutes more, we can drive over close to the river, and I can get off this fucking floor and sit and talk with you like a human being. This floor is terrible, David. Don't you think it's time you bring the car into one of those places and put a vacuum cleaner in here. All the stuff you got on the floor back here is in my mouth already."

The old man was laughing and muttering in Italian and making spitting and gagging sounds as we drove over to the river and parked. He got off the floor, brushed himself off, and moved into the front seat besides me.

"I'll have to come up here again," I told him, "and I have to spend more time with you. I can't remember all these names you're giving me and Funzi and Sally and Gigi aren't good enough names. I'll have to bring you pictures from the files downtown of all the KG's and hoods up here, and maybe you'll be able to pick these guys out so we'll know their real names.

"I've got some plate numbers. When we stopped at the light on 116th Street, I got about six numbers. I got the bronze Lincoln. But I'm going to have to come back and get all the plate numbers I can get. Then we'll check downtown and see who these cars belong to, and we can start to get home addresses for some of these bastards."

"We need all that?" the old man asked.

"Sure," I said.

"Just to lock up Ernie Boy? You need all that?"

"I'll lock up Ernie Boy. But who the fuck is Ernie Boy? He's

just moving packages. I lock up Ernie Boy and there's another Ernie Boy. I want the guys he's working for, every fucking one of them."

"You're kidding yourself, David. An Armando you can't
lock up. He's too high up. Nunzi is too high up. And don't
forget, David, you've got bad cops up here. The cops are
doing things with these people. They're making money with
them. I told you the cop that's selling guns? You know what
I mean, David? Maybe you can lock up an Ernie Boy. I'm
hoping. But you go after big people and you're going to have
trouble. From them and from cops. Just worry about Ernie
Boy. That's all I'm asking for."

"We've got to spend a whole day together," I told the old
man. "When can we do that?"

"Tomorrow is no good. I work Saturday. Sunday I'm off.
Sunday would be good."

We agreed to meet Sunday afternoon on a traffic island
near the off ramp of the Triboro Bridge connecting Manhattan with the Bronx and Queens.

The old man was standing just where he said he would be
when I came by to pick him up.

He quickly got into the car. I drove down a street under the
bridge and parked. "What's the matter, David? You're fifteen
minutes late," the old man joked. "Can't get up in the morning, huh? Just like my Vinnie."

The old man rubbed the palms of his hands together. "It's
cold, but at least this time I get to sit in the car with you and
I don't have to lay on the floor. You got the heat on? My friend
Angelo's brother from Rockaway just got a new car, a Buick,
you turn the key and in two seconds, you could be in the
North Pole and you got heat. In Rockaway, by the ocean, with
the wind this time of year, you need a car like that."

I opened the glove compartment, found a notebook and

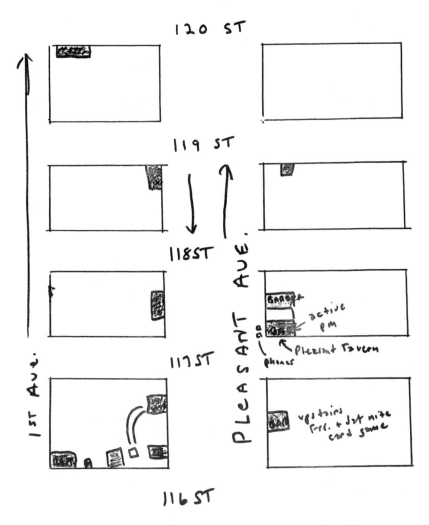

First map. This is the first crude map prepared by the old man on heroin activities along Pleasant Avenue. Most of the activity he knew about took place between 116th and 118th Streets. Each shaded area was a storefront social club or bar where the old man said heroin dealers met.

February 25, 1969

From: Det David Durk

To: Lt Lawrence Dempsey

Subject: ILLICIT SALE OF GUNS BY MEMBER OF FORCE

1. Confidential informant states that on February 5, 1969 at
approximately 10 PM in the Delightful Restaurant, 116 St-1st Ave,
he witnessed the sale of guns by a MOF to one "Ernie Boy" known to
the informant as a distributor of narcotics. He says that the
price was $100 each for two S&W .38 Special, $90 each for two .32
calibre "crack type" and price unknown for one .25 cal. automatic.
MOF is described as 5'8, 155 (thin), half bald, salt and pepper
swept back hair, maroon suit jacket, black pants, black raincoat.
MOF is frequently seen with gamblers and shylocks...,

Part of an early memo. After the first meetings with the old man,
this memorandum was put on file in the Department of Investigation. The confidential informant mentioned in the memo is, of
course, the old man. "MOF" means Member of the Force (a police
officer).

a pencil, and gave them to the old man.

"You've got to diagram everything. We'll make charts and
list everybody you know who's moving big packages, and
you've got to show me who's picking up for whom. I've got
to know one Funzi from another. And you've got to help me
draw a map of all the busy places on First Avenue, 116th
Street, and Pleasant Avenue. We've got to put down every
place you say there's action."

As the old man and I began writing, snowflakes started to
land on the car windshield. In a few minutes, it was snowing
so heavily we could have been parked right outside Nunzi's
luncheonette and nobody would have seen us.

For four hours, we sat in the cold car making maps and
charts. I began to feel that I had some understanding of the
street life and the relationships the old man wanted me to

know about. I would never again mistake Bath Beach Funzi for Funzi of 118th Street.

Neither of us complained about the cold. We weren't sitting in Angelo's brother's new Buick, but we were doing something we both knew to be important, and the feeling was good.

As I left the old man that evening, I was eager to get to my office the following morning and to get authorization to work full-time on the old man's information.

2. Department of Investigation

THE WITNESS: There hasn't been a mayor in this city, as far
               as I know, in the last one hundred years,
               who ever wanted to take on the police
               department face to face, knock-down
               drag-out battle. I don't recall one. . . .
QUESTION: The mayor has a real tough time.
THE WITNESS: That's right.
QUESTION: And that goes, I take it, you are saying for
               the Commissioner of Investigation?
THE WITNESS: Oh, I'm the mayor's man. . . .

  —Arnold Guy Fraiman
    Former New York City Commissioner of
    Investigation, testifying in closed
    session before the Knapp Commission, June 16, 1971

In February, 1969, I was one of sixteen NYC Police Department detectives and superior officers on special assignment to the city's Department of Investigation, an agency independent of the police department. I had worked for Commissioner Fraiman for three years and then, when Fraiman resigned to become a judge, I continued on working for the new commissioner, Fraiman's former deputy, Robert Ruskin.

Under the New York City charter, the Department of Investigation has very broad authority. It can investigate any allegation of corruption, inefficiency, or wrongdoing in the city government.

But, there was little I could do with the old man's information without getting authorization from Ruskin. He would have to make an official case out of it and assign me to it. That's what I hoped he would do even though I had no hard evidence of narcotics dealings. The old man's information was just that—information not evidence. But I did have a serious allegation involving a cop selling guns, and the old man had given me the name of the cop. I checked him out and found he was indeed assigned to the 25th Precinct in East Harlem. Also, I made my own observations. Cars were double- and triple-parked all over First Avenue and Pleasant Avenue while the local cops did nothing about it. I asked for an appointment with Ruskin and went in to see him.

I told Ruskin about my meetings with the old man. I began by saying that I had an informant who was giving me information on possible high-level narcotics dealings in the 25th Precinct in East Harlem. I also told Ruskin I had information on a cop who was possibly selling guns. And I told him local cops didn't seem to patrol East Harlem in the vicinity of Pleasant Avenue.

Ruskin listened closely and, when I finished my report, he said. "Sounds good. Terrific stuff, if it's true."

I was heartened. "Can I work on it on an official case basis."

"Not really," Ruskin answered.

"What do you mean? Not really?" I asked.

"Well."

"Well, what?"

"Well, David, you have to understand. If we work on it on an official case basis without turning what we have over to the police commissioner or the first deputy, it will appear we can't trust the Narcotics Division to investigate this thing. Do we want to give that kind of impression this early in the game?"

I protested. "If we turn over the whole case, it could be burned and my informant taken care of. You know it and I know it."

"David, don't worry. The case won't be burned. I will give it directly to Leary, commissioner to commissioner. That way nobody will dare burn it."

I left Ruskin's office with mixed feelings. Ruskin said he would talk directly to Police Commissioner Howard Leary. I knew Ruskin was making a proper referral. That was something. But what would Leary do? Who would he turn it over to? I had reason not to trust some of the men close to Leary. From other cases, I knew they weren't much interested in pursuing allegations of police corruption.

I was concerned about the old man's safety. I didn't want any cops in the 25th Precinct to know there was an investigation going on. I was concerned about the Narcotics Division getting involved. There were rumors of corruption in the Narcotics Division. If Ruskin had to turn the case over to the police department, it was best he take it right to the commissioner, but it would have been better by far if he allowed me to work the case myself, with detectives of my own choosing.

The Department of Investigation had never worked a narcotics case or an allegation of gun dealing in the police department. But, why not? If the information was serious enough for Ruskin to take it right to the police commissioner, why couldn't the D of I work the case itself? I waited, wondering what Leary would do.

Several days later, Ruskin told me that he had talked with Leary and that detectives were coming over from the Narcotics Division to talk with me. The men would be from SIU, the

Special Investigations Unit, an elite group of handpicked detectives who were assigned to major case work.

The SIU guys came over to see me at the D of I and I met with them in Ruskin's office. The ranking officer was Inspector James Lane, and with him were Detectives Robert Leuci and Gene D'Arpe.

We got off to a bad start. Lane asked me what I had of a specific nature. I told him that I had license plate numbers of suspects and had been down to the department's Bureau of Criminal Identification to see if any of the plate numbers checked out to individuals with criminal records. I told Lane that I had checked a small number of plates and several were indeed issued to known hoodlums and rackets guys.

"Durk, don't you know you don't have to go down to BCI and check files. That's a waste of your time. You can call in the information, and BCI will check the files for you," Inspector Lane told me.

"I don't like to do that, inspector."

I told Lane I had worked in the Chief Inspector's Confidential Investigating Unit, and one of the things we were told there was never to trust the clerical men who worked in BCI.

"You could be talking to a corrupt guy in BCI, inspector, and he could burn your case out just like that. If I'm interested in pulling some wiseguy file, I want to pull it myself. I don't want anybody else knowing about it. How do I know the clerk in BCI doesn't have a buddy in the 25th Precinct?"

Lane's face reddened. I later learned that Lane was a former commander of BCI, and there I was questioning the integrity of some of the men who used to work for him.

Leuci and D'Arpe asked me about specific locations. I showed them the crude map the old man and I had made of Pleasant Avenue. I told them my informant said that locations on Pleasant had passageways leading clear through to First Avenue. I told them about Nunzi's luncheonette and the passageway that was supposed to be behind a row of shelves there. And I gave them the address of an empty storefront where the old man said heroin was processed and bagged sometimes for street sales.

Every time I mentioned a location Leuci or D'Arpe wanted to know more about it. They wanted to know if I knew when heavy loads of junk moved out of each place. I said I didn't.

I said I had just begun to meet with my informant and that I didn't have much specific information beyond locations, a few plate numbers, and street names of suspected dealers.

Inspector Lane said, "What you got, Durk, is general intelligence. I could get this kind of stuff in the squad room of any station house."

Leuci and D'Arpe looked very interested. They hardly looked over at Lane when he talked, and they were writing as fast as they could, copying my charts and my map of Pleasant Avenue. Lane seemed annoyed with me. Later, I learned Lane had been told to be very careful in his dealings with me. Another cop got information to Lane that I might use the narcotics information primarily to make corruption cases against cops or to embarrass the Narcotics Division.

"Durk is a motherfucker," Lane was told. "He's the one guy in this squad who I'm sure would lock up another cop."

On his way out of the building, Lane turned to the detectives with him and Leuci remembers him saying, "I'm going to tell you something. I don't trust him."

Whatever feelings Lane had about me, he did take the information seriously and I was invited over to SIU a few days later. The SIU offices were on the third floor of the First Precinct stationhouse near the Fulton Fish Market in lower Manhattan. It was my first visit to SIU, and it was like going to a CIA safehouse for the first time. SIU was so secret that many cops didn't know it existed. The commanding officer of the unit was Captain Daniel Tange, a handsome man and one of the youngest captains in the department.

Tange's demeanor was not very different from Lane's. He stood four or five feet from me in the middle of a big squad room and looked at me with suspicion. Tange said he knew I had gone to Ruskin with narcotics information and Ruskin had gone to Leary. He said he couldn't understand why a detective in the Department of Investigation, not assigned to narcotics, was going out of his way to develop information on heavy narcotics dealings.

"Who's your informant, Durk? Bring him up here! How do you come to have information on major violators? You just meet a guy, and he's giving you stuff like this? Nobody just walks into information on the heavy stuff. Listen, Durk, either you bring your informant up here or stop wasting our time."

I said I wouldn't produce the old man without assurances that I could work the case and that he would be safeguarded. Tange waved his finger at me. "You listen to me, Durk. I'm a captain and you're a detective. If you ever do anything to embarrass this command, I'll have your back broken."

It was all unreal. First Lane took off at me, and now it was Tange's turn.

What Tange said and how he said it shocked me. Why all the hostility? I sat on a desk top and looked around the room while Tange continued to stare at me. I noticed that SIU had copied my charts. The information I had given Lane was now all neatly laid out in India ink on big easel cards. And the cards were neatly arranged on the desk of Lieutenant Gabriel Stefania, Tange's chief aide.

My eyes fixed on the charts. I was bewildered. There was no logic to what was happening. Captain Tange was trying to talk me off what might be a major investigation. Leuci and D'Arpe hadn't said so, but I sensed that they took the old man's information very seriously, and I knew they were both highly respected street cops.

What was it all about? Why was Tange up the wall? Did he resent me coming to him under the aegis of the police commissioner? Was he worried that, if I had something good, credit would go to the D of I, not to the Narcotics Division? Or was there more to it than that? Why would Tange risk coming down so hard on me if he didn't really have to?

It was all so damned illogical. I didn't have the patience for it. The old man wanted me to lock up Ernie Boy. If his information was really good, I could team up with hot shots like Leuci and D'Arpe, who knew all the Funzis, and maybe we could lock up guys with hundreds of kilos of heroin. I looked out across the SIU squad room. Tange had his back to me now, and detectives stood around the room in twos and threes talking quietly. Too quietly. I didn't know whether I was expected to stay or to leave. As I started for the door, Leuci looked up from something he was reading.

"Wait a minute, Durk," he called to me. Leuci looked over at Tange, who was not looking in our direction, and walked over to me. Leuci was of medium height, stockily built. He had dark wavy hair and a mustache. Although very intense, his manner was friendly.

"Listen, Durk, I shouldn't even be talking to you, but I want to tell you something. Don't put your heart in this one."

Leuci confirmed my suspicions—something was horribly wrong in SIU. He didn't have to say more. With a few words, he'd made me understand that SIU was playing games with me and that he thought I was in over my head. It was a very serious moment for both of us.

Bob Leuci wasn't ready that afternoon to tell me all that was wrong in SIU, but he gave me fair warning.

By warning me SIU wouldn't work with me, Leuci put a lot on the line. More than either of us could know then. Those words, "Durk, don't put your heart in this one," and the way Bob said them, were to stick in my mind. And, later, much later, I reached out for Bob Leuci to level with me and with himself about corruption in SIU. And he did. By then, we both knew he didn't belong with the wiseguys he had fallen in with. The shield said "City of New York" and that was the side Bob wanted to be on.

3. The Heroin Code

In their street talk, addicts and pushers have many names for heroin. Among blacks in Harlem, heroin is junk or dope or shit. In Cuban or Puerto Rican neighborhoods, it's *la stuffa* or *la heroina*. Typically, a Puerto Rican addict will be in the street looking to buy *una cuchara de la stuffa*—a spoonful of heroin. The Italian street word for heroin, *babyn,* is rarely spoken.

The major Italian heroin dealers have a special way of talking when they are doing business. They would never use words like *babyn* or junk or dope or—God forbid—heroin. Large drug transactions are conducted in code.

In the code used in the late 1960s, the heroin dealers sounded like buyers of children's wear for Sears or Macy's. On the phone, they talked endlessly about articles of children's clothing—about socks and shoes and pants and shirts.

In the language of a Pleasant Avenue dealer, a boy's shirt meant a kilo of heroin. A girl's shirt was a kilo of cocaine. The code was carefully adhered to, but even when the heroin dealers on The Avenue were trying to be cautious in their dealings, they often made clear what they were really talking about. Federal agents who listened in on narcotics wiretaps remember many revealing moments. For example, one agent remembers a phone conversation between an out-of-town heroin buyer and an East Harlem dealer. The buyer began the conversation:

"Hey, is that you? This is me."

"Yeah. Hello. What do you need?"

"I got my cousin here from Toledo."

"Yeah."

"You got boys' shirts?"

"I got. I got."

"You sure you got?"

"Would I tell you yes, if I didn't?"

"You got boys' shirts? [no answer] Are they white? [pure]"

"Sure they're white. Did you ever get shirts from me that weren't white? You *gavon.*"

"Are they fresh?"

"What do you mean are they fresh? Listen, you sonofabitch, you want shirts, I got. Do you want to order, or do you want to play with yourself all day?"

"All right, all right, wait a minute. [Hushed voices away from phone] All right, my cousin says we'll take half a shirt."

The men who processed and distributed more than half of this country's heroin supply began working out of fixed locations on Pleasant Avenue in East Harlem sometime in the late 1940s. For them, it was "The Avenue." They felt safer and more at home on The Avenue than anywhere else. In the warmer months, the old man told me, you could see the heroin bosses in undershirts and T-shirts getting in and out of Cadillacs and Lincolns on their way from one storefront heroin operation to another. Capra, Zanfardino and the other men who controlled the heroin business were surrounded by young hoods on their way up like Ernie Boy and by *larbos* (ass-kissers), older neighborhood guys trying to get to do odd jobs for the big men. The *larbos* would serve as chauffeurs on a trip to Jersey for a sitdown (important meeting), or they'd be sent around the corner to Patsy's on First Avenue for pizza, but they would never be trusted to move packages of heroin or to handle money.

If the moguls of the heroin establishment were going to talk business, the *larbos* knew enough to leave the storefront social clubs and go outside on the sidewalk and play dominoes.

If nothing big was going on, if there were no sitdowns, if no large shipments were expected or being worked in the cutting mills, the *larbos* would be lounging in the storefronts and the major heroin figures wouldn't be seen.

But if an important shipment was expected, the bosses and the Cadillacs and the Lincolns would be everywhere. The long limos would be double- and triple-parked day and night. And yet, SIU detectives insisted they could not find the limos which would be there almost every night. And hundreds of pounds of heroin would be moving out to the Bronx, Brooklyn, Jersey, and points west—Detroit, St. Louis, Atlanta, Toledo.

Between midnight and dawn, night after night, millions of dollars would change hands on The Avenue.

And, while the cash transactions were going on, the cutters, the baggers, the people who processed heroin for street sale would be working all night in tenement apartments above the busy storefront social clubs.

During the 1960s, Pleasant Avenue was a street that never closed down. If you knew the right people, you could go there at three in the morning and borrow fifty thousand dollars in cash or rent a submachine gun or arrange to fix a judge or pick up three kilos of heroin.

The processing of heroin on The Avenue was a kitchen-table, cottage industry that employed hundreds of neighborhood men and women who worked day and night turning out tons of packaged heroin.

Years before, Italian immigrants sat all day at their kitchen tables turning out embroidery. Now their children and grandchildren turned out heroin. They often worked thirteen to fifteen hours at a time in an apartment where the temperature could be in the nineties. But no window could be opened, no air conditioner could be turned on. The heroin dealers didn't want their precious powder blowing around somebody's kitchen, and heroin dust in the air would make the workers high just as if they were snorting. The heroin, processed in Corsican laboratories in Marseilles, was brought to the cutting tables usually a quarter kilo at a time. It was "pure" heroin. On the kitchen tables the heroin, which had arrived in the country earlier that day or the night before, would be mixed with milk sugar and repackaged. Quarter-kilo bags of 80 percent purity became half-kilo bags of 40 percent purity.

Many of the old man's neighbors on Pleasant Avenue worked as heroin cutters and baggers. And others who didn't rented out their apartments at certain hours for the cutters to come in and work.

The old man remembered the kitchen table where his mother had worked piece-goods embroidery and where he had sat writing up records for loan sharking and numbers, but he didn't want his son, Vinnie, moving heroin packages for Nunzi and the other wiseguys in the social clubs.

"You know my father, David, was a real *gavon.* He didn't give a shit about me. He was a greaseball. If I came home at two, three in the morning, he didn't care. He didn't care about his children.

"But with me and my wife, it's different. My wife was an orphan. To her, having her own children and being a mother to them is everything. And I know what it was, not having a father. I want my kids to know they have a father, a real father.

"And, David, when you're trying to really be a father, when you know how your wife has tried, and a kid starts talking how my Vinnie is talking, it really hurts.

"My kid brother needed eight thousand dollars for a brain operation. You know what my father did? He took off. All of a sudden, he couldn't hide in the bar any longer. He had to come up with the eight thousand, so he couldn't take the pressure and took off.

"Well, now my kid Vinnie needs a brain operation. He's got to get heroin hustling out of his head, and I don't want to duck this. My father ducked plenty. But I don't want to duck this, David."

By March of 1969, the old man and I would be meeting for calzone or manicotti two or three times a week. He'd give me new license plate numbers to check and the latest talk of the street. One time he told me that heroin was stashed in a bakery on First Avenue. Another week it would be in Astoria or up in the Bronx. Generally, big shipments would come in on Tuesday or Wednesday and then be worked and ready for the street on the weekend.

The old man was growing impatient with me. I had promised to bring him pictures of known hoodlums from the department's intelligence files, but I'd not been able to get access to the right files. I kept promising him something would be done with the information he was giving me, but days went by and I could report nothing solid.

"David, if anybody should know I'm talking to you, you don't know how bad it would be for me. When they get a guy like me, they don't just shoot him. I remember what they did to Whitey Marsh's cousin. He didn't even rat out anybody. All he did was pay for a load with some counterfeit. And they found his body with his arms off and a cherry bomb up his ass.

Ernie Boy on The Avenue. This picture of Abbamonte was taken by a detective working the Operation Window detail. "I don't want to hear any more about Ernie Boy," the old man told me when we first talked. "All I want is you should get him good with the stuff and he should sit in Rikers [prison] . . . and wear out his pants."

"Be careful, David, for both of us. Life doesn't mean anything to these guys. They would torture me for a week before putting a bullet in me, just to make an example."

Oreste "Ernie Boy" Abbamonte was *the* neighborhood delivery boy. Barely old enough to buy a drink legally in a bar, Ernie Boy was regularly moving heroin packages worth tens of thousands of dollars.

He saw himself as "a real comer" and he strutted along The Avenue with the swagger of a Mafia *consiglieri,* often counting money—usually a roll of fifties. And he was active in recruiting other neighborhood kids to work as runners in the heroin operations of his boss, Gennaro Zanfardino. Among neighborhood toughs, Ernie Boy was *the* success story of Pleasant Avenue.

"If you could put that fucking kid where he belongs, David, maybe my Vinnie would get the message."

Narcotics cases are not easily made. Successful felony prosecutions in drug cases almost always are based on painstaking police work—on wiretaps and on extensive surveillance and undercover work. It is difficult to catch the Ernie Boys in the act of moving a package. Ernie Boy might be called upon to work only twenty minutes a day, and that twenty minutes at five o'clock in the morning. It is just as difficult to hear the Zanfardinos and Capras talk about anything but shoes and socks and shirts and pants.

I wanted nothing more than to be assigned to the case and to catch Ernie Boy in the act of moving a package. I wanted the old man to have his miracle, and I wanted to stop the flow of heroin out of Pleasant Avenue.

But time passed and I was not assigned to the case. No one was assigned to the case. So far as I knew, there was no case. The SIU bosses would not return my calls, and my bosses at the Department of Investigation refused to ask the police commissioner why nothing was happening.

Detectives at SIU were too busy to talk to me. I later found out why.

4. Special Investigations Unit

"Why you running after me, driving me crazy? What am I, some nigger? You think I'll ever wait for you in a doorway with two other guys and shoot you? Let me do business, and a year from now I promise you, I'll poison a package and kill a thousand of those fuckers."

—Excerpt from tape of Mafia heroin dealer talking to an SIU detective in Harlem shortly after riots touched off by the assassination of Martin Luther King, Jr., April 4, 1968

As it unfolded in later investigations, the story of SIU is that of men who were poor in their twenties, rich in their thirties, and under indictment (or in jail) in their forties. One former SIU detective captured the spirit of the place when he later confessed, "SIU was like a beautiful woman. It was fascinating. You got to work with the best cops on the best cases. And where else could guys like us, guys from Corona, Astoria, Ozone Park, guys who never even went to college, where else could we ever get to make so much money?"

It's a story of policemen growing up in the go-go years of the 1950s and 1960s and listening to the couch talk of cousins and brothers-in-law who were making it in real estate or the stockmarket or in the funny-money world of the large corporations. It's a story of men working for the city for eighteen thousand dollars a year and suddenly finding out how to make eighteen thousand a night.

By 1969, SIU and much of the New York City Police Department's Narcotics Division had become a kind of heroin brokerage. The heroin establishment—the Italian, Cuban, and South American multi-kilo dealers—were all but running narcotics law enforcement in the city. The major SIU cases were most often made when the establishment wanted them made. The big dealers got rid of competition by giving up smaller dealers to the police.

In 1970, SIU, a unit of only seventy men, seized more heroin and other illicit drugs than were seized by all customs, border patrol, and federal narcotics agents working throughout the country.

But no one was looking too closely at how these seizures were made or at what happened to the seized narcotics. Detectives who were later indicted for corruption were breaking one big case after another. How they did it was their business.

This was the heyday of SIU. It was steak or lobster every night. Cops who grew up in row houses in Jackson Heights were now moving out to split-level homes in suburbia. The cops had money, their wives and girl friends had money, children went to sleep-away camps, and detectives joked with one another about hiring armored cars to take them home at night. Officers who were ripping off narcotics dealers generally carried self-addressed, stamped envelopes with them for making "night deposits" in the mailbox soon after seizing large sums of money.

As detectives, they were good. They knew all the Funzis, all the street people, all the meeting places, and by using illegal wiretaps, so-called gypsy wires, they were resourceful enough to catch dealers with shipments of heroin even when other dealers didn't tip them off.

At first, taking only money, they turned in seized drugs.

And they weren't uptight about it. Sergeants and lieutenants were told about what was going on and were given their cut. Detectives found themselves saying, "What better way to hurt the bastards than to take their money? Why leave it for the lawyers and the bailsmen? Why turn it in to the city? What was Lindsay going to do with it? Give it out in welfare and put more money into Harlem for junk?"

SIU detectives liked the street action. They liked the money but had only contempt for the system. For them the mayor, the courts, the lawyers, the judges, and the long-delayed trials were all bullshit. It was better, they thought, to hold court in the street and to act out their version of Robin Hood and his merrie men of Sherwood Forest. For, after all, they could put the money to better use than either the city or the pushers.

When I first walked into SIU, I knew little about the men who worked there, and they knew little about me. But what they knew was enough. The department wire* had it that Durk couldn't be trusted. He was the kind of cop who would lock up anyone, even other cops. He wouldn't play the game.

I later found out that word was passed that SIU was not to cooperate with me. Assistant Chief Inspector Thomas Renaghan, then chief of the Narcotics Division, a cop with thirty years on the job, put it bluntly to one of his detectives: "Durk is a hoppel. I want him out of here, and I want him out of here fast."

Captain Tange ordered that no detective in SIU was to talk to me without a boss (a superior officer) present. And Tange made inquiries among his best street detectives. He tested the waters. Could Durk's information be worked without Durk and without Durk's informant? One detective said yes. Gypsy wires could be put on some of the Pleasant Avenue

---

*The grapevine. In this case, it was an easy matter for cops in SIU to call cops in the D of I to find out what kind of guy I was.

people Durk said were dealers. There would be no need for court orders. It would all be off the books, on spec. But Tange was hesitant.

SIU was well aware that there was a gambling and numbers pad on Pleasant Avenue. The investigation could get out of hand even without Durk. And one SIU detective recalls a commander saying, "I don't want Narcotics Division locking up cops for doing things with KG's."

The first specific information I had about widespread heroin racketeering among policemen came from the old man, and it involved Ernie Boy.

Abbamonte, according to the old man, was driving uptown one afternoon moving a three-pound package of heroin. Narcotics detectives who had him under surveillance stopped the car, searched it, and found the stuff along with two pistols and a shotgun. Ernie Boy was brought to the 25th Precinct station house in East Harlem, but he wasn't arrested. Instead, the old man said, Ernie Boy was told to have his people bring ransom money to the squad room.

In a few hours, the Pleasant Avenue heroin dealers had sent in seventy thousand dollars to the detectives. Once they had their ransom money, the detectives told Ernie Boy that he could leave with his three pounds of heroin—but no guns.

Ernie Boy protested. "I can't go out on the street with three pounds of stuff and no guns. Somebody will rip me off for the stuff, and my people won't like that after they sent over all that money."

The detectives thought it over. Seventy thousand was nice money, and they didn't want any trouble from Abbamonte's people.

When Ernie Boy left, he left with the heroin and one gun. Sometime later a narcotics detective who worked East Harlem told me, "That's all bullshit, David. What do you mean seventy thousand. It wasn't seventy. It was fifty thousand."

By 1969, there were two major marketing operations of heroin in New York City. One operated out of Pleasant Avenue; the other operated out of the fourth floor of the First Precinct station house in lower Manhattan—the headquarters of the Special Investigations Unit of the police department's Narcotics Division.

If a middle-level drug dealer wanted to buy a kilo of heroin in New York, he could buy it from a Mafia dealer on Pleasant Avenue—or from a cop assigned to SIU.

In the late 1960s and in the early 1970s, New York City policemen sold hundreds of kilos of heroin and cocaine. The greater horror is that the top command of the New York City Police Department was warned by federal investigators as early as 1969 that as many as seventy New York City detectives were suspected of dealing in drugs. The names of the suspected detectives were supplied by a federal narcotics agent who was himself caught dealing large quantities of heroin. But the information from the Feds was virtually ignored. Attached to the Feds' written requests for assistance in investigating suspects was a note in which the top anticorruption official and closest associate to First Deputy Commissioner John Walsh wrote: "First Deputy Commissioner doesn't want to help the feds lock up local police. Let them arrest Federal people."

There were thieves and drug dealers serving in one of the city's most sensitive police units and the men who ran the department didn't want to know about it and the mayor's people didn't want to know. They didn't want to know about it from the federal government and, as I learned more and more about the horrible secret, they didn't want to know about it from me.

Narcotics law enforcement in the city of New York had been taken over by criminals within the department—and narcotics law enforcement became just as dirty a business as street dealing in narcotics.

The heroin business flourished in New York because of the enormous profits it generated for the dealers on the street and for corrupt policemen and public officials. SIU detectives played a running cat-and-mouse game with Latin heroin and cocaine dealers who made frequent trips to New York from Colombia and Chile. To be sure, few of these dealers were arrested, and fewer still convicted. But many lost their drugs, money, and expensive jewelry to SIU club members.

Typically, six or seven Chilean drug dealers would arrive at Kennedy International Airport and drive to an apartment in the Jackson Heights section of Queens. They would set up shop and sell drugs for three or four days. SIU guys would be sitting on the apartment waiting for the dealers to head back to the airport with their profits.

The dealers would try to be careful. Often they would take along children and girl friends, and the money might be hidden in a child's Crackerjack box, in stuffed toys, or in vaginas. But the SIU men were resourceful. If they smelled money, they looked in all the probable and improbable places.

A whole etiquette of corruption developed. If a team of detectives scored money from heroin dealers at an airport or a hotel, each team member would get an equal share, and the team's sergeant and lieutenant would each get a share and a half or a double share.

Word got around among the wiseguys and hustlers in the department that SIU was *the* place to work. SIU became a rich and elitist crime family. The SIU guys were the best con men, the best wiretappers, the best burglars, the best stickup men, the best shakedown artists. And they knew New York better than any cabdriver or pickpocket. They had little to worry about.

As one detective would say later, "Who'd ever get to know what my partner and I did with some junk dealer at three o'clock in the morning in a hallway in Harlem?"

SIU hustlers knew that on occasion they might be followed by the police commissioner's confidential squad or members of other corruption control units. Some of these headquarters shooflies were known to be good men who could not be bought off. If they caught SIU guys in the act of a shakedown, it could be a bad scene.

But the men in SIU were street wise and cocky. They knew that many of the commissioner's men were studying for advanced degrees in police science or administration. Leuci would later joke about it. "How could they work a twenty-four-hour tail [surveillance]?" he said with a grin. "For Christ's sake, they'd be falling asleep in class."

If the SIU guys worried about anything, they worried about the sadists and clowns in the unit who might cause trouble by their lack of restraint. Within the unit, there was an effort to keep those guys in line. Lower-level street dealers—particularly blacks—who resisted shakedowns were often worked over. A black dealer who wasn't "cooperating" might be locked in a car trunk, and left there for several hours. When a dealer "really had to be taught a lesson," a snake was put in the car trunk with him. One detective would say to another, "Let the nigger think it over for a while."

An objecting detective might say, "You shouldn't do that. That nigger is going to get back out on the street, and he's not going to like us."

The detective with the key to the trunk would say "fuck 'em," and that was that. The guys who put dealers in car trunks were considered psychos, and their tactics were considered crude and dangerous. In SIU you didn't rock the boat. You did your own thing, together with your partner or your team, and you left the other guys alone.

Each team had its own style and its own ways of scoring

heroin money. How they made cases was their business. The
SIU bosses didn't want to know.

Frequently, SIU cops formed alliances with certain heroin
street dealers in order to rip off other dealers.

A former SIU detective gives this accounting of how such
an alliance would work:

> We'd know that two guys were dealing heavy, say, on the
> same block in West Harlem and buying from the same
> supplier. We'd go to one guy and offer him a deal if he'd
> give us the other guy. The first guy might tell us to go fuck
> ourselves. But, also, he might think about it and see that if
> he worked with us two things would happen for him. First,
> we'd get rid of some of his competition for him and,
> number two, nothing would be said, but he'd get the
> message that we wouldn't come after him—at least for a
> while. He could stay in business. You know, he could keep
> renting the sidewalk from the city.
>
> So, once we get a guy's head right and get him working
> with us, then we just wait until the shipment of junk comes
> in. The both guys are on the same block picking up from
> the same supplier. When the first guy has, when he's dirty,
> the second guy is going to be dirty, too. So, we grab the
> second guy and we get the stuff. And, if the seizure is
> good, just to show the first guy it pays to work with us,
> maybe we throw him a quarter of kilo on the arm.
>
> Now, the second guy who we lock up will be sitting in
> the can dying to know who gave him up. Now, we can
> score this bastard, too. We throw him a name of the guy
> who ratted him out—not the right name, of course, but a
> name from the neighborhood. And the name will be good
> for two or three grand. Sometimes more.
>
> Now, the guy whose name you give out is going to get a
> bullet in the head from the guy you locked up. That you
> can bet on. So you make sure you finger the worst
> motherfucker you could think of.
>
> Oh, and I almost forgot, the guy you lock up is going to

want to fix up his case in court so then the bastard is
going to have to come up with some more bread, but
that's another story. But you get the idea, the thing is
beautiful. It just goes around and around and everybody is
handing you money, and we're hurting the bastards real
good.

It was a Malice-in-Wonderland world for the SIU guys and
practically every night was New Year's Eve.

After a few months in SIU, cash-laden detectives would
become regular customers at the Canal Street jewelry
stores, and girl friends and wives and mothers, who were
used to rhinestones, would start to get birthday presents like
they never saw before. SIU money went south to be invested
in Florida motels. And, if there was a shortage of safe deposit
boxes in town, the SIU guys had a lot to do with it.

The seventy-odd detectives in SIU were on a roller-coaster
ride that would end in tragedy for most of them. Those wild
nights of scoring heroin dealers would lead to indictments,
suicides, broken marriages, and destroyed lives. Partners in
SIU who were buddies for years would take the stand to
testify against each other. And all that money in all those
safe-deposit boxes would go for lawyers and psychiatrists,
and for back taxes and IRS fines.

But in that spring of 1969, the guys in SIU didn't know that
it would all end up that way. And I didn't know either. I just
knew that Leuci and the others at SIU were on orders not to
talk to me and that the department was not taking action
against the men who drove the Lincolns and Cadillacs on
Pleasant Avenue.

The old man was waiting for some good news from me, but
for some time he heard no good news. He sat at his domino
game on Pleasant Avenue and heard more of the same talk,
the same talk about junk. And he watched Ernie Boy crossing

back and forth on The Avenue. And one Sunday, while the old man was playing dominoes, a little boy in a communion suit came walking by on his way from church, and Ernie Boy called to him and gave him some money. The kid looked at the money and said, "Gee, mister, ten dollars, thanks." The old man listened and wondered how long it would be before his son Vinnie was throwing ten-dollar bills to kids in communion suits along Pleasant Avenue.

5. Seventh Avenue Dealers

For years, the Stage Delicatessen on Seventh Avenue in midtown Manhattan has had a loyal clientele of show-biz and garment-industry old-timers who wouldn't think of talking business without munching on four-dollar, overstuffed pastrami sandwiches, pickles, and sour tomatoes. And the Stage's devotees swear by Dr. Brown's Celery Tonic, plain over ice, which everybody knows soothes the gastric juices. With Dr. Brown's on the table, who needs Alka Seltzer?

In the late 1960s, two New York businessmen dined at the Stage almost every day. For Herbie Sperling and Sonny Gold business was heroin, wholesale only. The tables at the Stage, the sidewalk outside, a barbershop down the block, and the nearby Gold Rail Bar, were all places where they met to discuss business. That's where the black and Spanish kilo-buyers could find Sperling and Gold and other members of the Jewish Mafia. They sunned themselves along a two-block stretch of Seventh Avenue and felt as safe there as the Capras and Zanfardinos felt on Pleasant Avenue.

Among the heroin wholesalers of Seventh Avenue, Sperling was the boss. He was in competition with the Italians on Pleasant Avenue, but he got along with them quite well. And they helped each other out. On a busy Saturday, if Sperling was running low on inventory, he could always get on the phone and call Pleasant Avenue for a few shirts. Or he could send Gold uptown to look for a *shabbos goy* on The Avenue who might have a loose kilo.

Sperling's mother had an apartment on Eighth Avenue, about three blocks from the Stage. The mother was about as communicative as a Sioux Indian in the days of Custer, and word had it that she spoke only to God. Federal agents believed that her apartment was a perfect place to leave packages for Herbie.

Sperling bought most of his heroin from a London dealer who got it directly from Corsican laboratories in Marseilles, but he also worked closely with Johnny Capra, Leo Guarino, and other Italians in East Harlem, who could be counted upon to supply heroin when shipments from abroad were delayed.

When Sperling was coming up on the Lower East Side, he had the reputation of being the meanest kid who ever walked down Delancey Street. When he went into the heroin business and became a major supplier to black dealers in Harlem, he had little trouble getting backing from Jewish moneymen in New York and Westchester. Sperling made "trading" in heroin a hot item in commodities futures, like platinum and hog bellies.

If you knew lawyers with the right connections who were "steerers" for Herbie, you could invest in the heroin market, and your investment would be strictly confidential and "off the books." One Sperling investor bragged to an undercover agent about all the money he was making from his Harlem investments. "Herbie's made me rich and who knows the difference? I've heard of him, but I've never met him and he never heard of me. God bless him, that little *mamser* Herbie."

The dealers who worked for Sperling were fond of hiring "guinea kids" from East Harlem to move packages for them. If a Capra or a Zanfardino or an Ernie Boy gave a kid from Pleasant Avenue the nod, it was like a letter from Jonas Salk recommending a boy for medical school.

And, tragically, for some of the best and the brightest among the East Harlem street kids, a Johnny Capra *was* Jonas Salk. Capra was a man you could look up to. And Capra was in a position to really help a sharp kid on the way up. You didn't have to have good marks from school. You didn't have to have a job resumé. If a kid had smarts, Capra would find out about him without having to check up on how the kid did in algebra.

And it wasn't long before Vinnie, the old man's son, came to the attention of the wiseguys on Pleasant Avenue. As the old man feared, it was Ernie Boy who made the introductions. And, before the old man or I could do anything about it, Vinnie was moving packages.

Like many typographers on big metropolitan dailies, the old man worked nights—often sitting at his Linotype machine until well after midnight. Then he'd scrub the ink from his hands, change into street clothes, and be ready to join his buddies from the composing room for a nightly beer in an Irish bar on West Forty-third. The old man had worked the same job and had lifted beers with the same men for years. They had no secrets. But now the old man had one.

When he'd get home to the top-floor walk-up apartment on Pleasant Avenue, he'd put up a pot of coffee and sit down to read the newspaper he and his buddies had just turned out.

He'd check Vinnie's room, and night after night Vinnie wouldn't be there. He'd sit and wait. He'd doze off and wake up, and Vinnie still wouldn't be there.

Sometimes it would be daylight before the old man would hear the key turning in the lock and then see his son walk right by the kitchen, right by his father, saying nothing.

"Hey, you blind?" the old man would shout after Vinnie. The old man would follow Vinnie into his room.

"Where you been all night? Tell your father where you
been all night."

"New Rochelle."

"What do you mean, New Rochelle? What's in New Rochelle?"

"A party."

"What kind of party all night on a Tuesday night?"

"Listen, Pop, you've been where you been and I've been
where I've been. Okay? How about we leave it just like that?"

" 'How about we leave it just like that,' that's what he tells
me, David. What should I do, punch him out in the mouth? Do
you think hitting kids does any good? What can I do, tie him
to the bed?

"He doesn't ask me for money anymore. He has his own
money. Plenty. I say to him, where are you getting all that
money? What did you become? A pimp, or a dope pusher?
And he laughs at me and says he has his own numbers
business like he knows I used to have. He says all I have to
do is say the word and he'll give me a piece of the action.
He'll give me 112th Street, he says. Some *gavon,* huh, David?"

Vinnie was moving heroin packages for months before the
old man heard about it from the *larbos* he played dominoes
with on The Avenue. "He's working for Jews from the
Bronx," the *larbos* said. The old man went looking for Vinnie.
There was a fight and Vinnie moved out of the apartment.

Vinnie was eighteen and full of energy. He could work
through the night making trips all over the city and still be in
good enough shape to have breakfast and a "matinee" with
one or more of the young girls who visited his new apartment
on East Eighty-first Street. He was snorting cocaine and
dropping bennies, buying shoes at mod boutiques on Third

Avenue and meeting girls, doing business and—moving, moving, moving. Life was good.

He'd punch Ernie Boy in the arm, dance around him, bob and weave, throw a punch and hug him. "Tell me the truth, Ernie," he'd ask, "who's better looking, me or Mikie Papa?"

Vinnie was learning the heroin business. He came to understand that the profits from loan sharking, bookmaking, numbers banking, or hijacking were nothing compared with the enormous sums to be made from dealing junk. And he came to understand that very few men had the financing, the know-how, and the connections to bring heroin into this country in large quantitites. He came to know that deals made in sitdowns on Pleasant Avenue controlled the flow of heroin worldwide.

He was sitting at the feet of kings. The Sperlings, the Capras, and the Zanfardinos controlled a substance more precious than gold. Hundreds of thousands of junkies in Harlem and Bed-Stuy, in Detroit and Toledo, in Newark and Watts would be running wild in the streets if it weren't for the few men in East Harlem and in the Bronx, those who knew how to get the stuff out day after day.

Vinnie couldn't sit with the high and mighty of the heroin business, not yet. But he could sit with the Ernie Boys, the Mikie Papas, and the other young hoods on their way up. On a slow Monday night, they'd get together at a back table in the Tambourine on East Eighty-first.

The bosses of the heroin business sat in old Pleasant Avenue storefronts at bridge tables in their undershirts, but their delivery boys wore eighty-dollar suede vests and sixty-dollar Swiss-made shoes. And the air around their table at the Tambourine was heavy with Patchoulli, Brut, and Aramis.

These kids grew up watching Sinatra and Sammy Davis and Mick Jagger and Sly Stone, and they were sure they knew all the special moves. They could turn on a chick they just met with just the right look and, more crucial to their heroin operations, they could hit it off quickly with blacks and Cubans and Puerto Ricans they were called upon to do business with on the street. The old Italians on The Avenue wouldn't trust a black racketeer unless they'd known him for years, but the Ernie Boys would deal with blacks they hardly knew—they felt they could size up a black dude, or any dude, in five minutes.

The boys at that back table in the Tambourine were restless and in a hurry. At eighteen, Vinnie thought the world was passing by the very men who were making him rich—the Zanfardinos and the Capras. The bosses were too conservative. Their heads were still in the old country—they were thinking and living as if they were still in Palermo.

The old Italians feared smooth-talking young blacks from the Caribbean since they could speak French with the Corsicans. But the Ernie Boys and Vinnies came to admire and trust some of the black dealers. "These cats got a lot of class," you could hear them say at the Tambourine. "You got to hand it to a nigger like Nicky Barnes or Black Zack. They can really work the street. They're buying kilos from us and doing their own cutting and packaging and controlling the action all the way down to the five-dollar bags on the street. Do you know what kind of bread that has to be? What does Capra make on a kilo? He cuts it once and deals it off. Maybe he's making twenty thou or thirty on a kilo. I betcha a sonofabitch like Black Zack or Rufus Boyd over in Brooklyn is making two hundred thousand ᴀ kilo by cutting and bagging it all the way to the street.

"The niggers know how to work heroin. But the guys you really got to watch are the Chinks. That rock junk they got down in Chinatown is dynamite. I'm telling you, give it five years and all the action is going to be down on Pell Street and over on Delancey. The Chinks have got the heavy boat connections and they are dealing it off direct to the Spics in Brooklyn. The Ricans are coming across that bridge for big sitdowns on Delancey and they are going back loaded.

"And half those Chink guys are married to Rican broads. And the Rican broads' families are putting it out in the street for the Chinks. They got control over everything. And, how long they been in this country? Now, come on, we gotta be doing better than we're doing.

"We couldn't put our hands on some heavy rock stuff if our life depended on it. And, if we need heavy coke, we got to go begging for it from the Spics in Jersey. That's bullshit. Either we got an operation or we're fucking playing games."

That kind of talk was all right for the Tambourine but not on The Avenue. Ernie Boy and Vinnie didn't say anything of the kind in front of Capra or the other established dealers.

The older Italians on Pleasant Avenue were in complete control of the business, and they took as few risks as possible. Pleasant Avenue was strictly a Mom-and-Pop store. If an Ernie Boy ever started talking about running a heroin operation the way black dealers were doing it, a Capra would tell him to shut up. Ernie Boy would be told that when you start getting into street dealing—into bags and spoons—you are asking for trouble.

The Capras settled for a profit of only twenty or thirty thousand on a kilo, but they were able to deal in relative anonymity. Few people outside of Pleasant Avenue knew who they were. In Harlem, hundreds of guys knew Nicky Barnes and Black Zack and J. C. Abrahams and Goldfinger and Spanish Raymond and other major street dealers. "The niggers take too many chances," the Pleasant Avenue dealers would say. The Capras supplied the big black dealers. They arranged for the blacks to buy kilos but, when the heroin was delivered, the major Italian dealers were nowhere near the scene. That's why the Ernie Boys and the Vinnies were hired to move packages. And that's why the Pleasant Avenue Moustache Petes had worked out elaborate schemes for the delivery of heroin to street dealers. Street dealers they trusted just so far, even after years of doing business with them.

The key figures in the Italian heroin establishment never touched heroin. Guys who were in the business for twenty years and had made millions off it had never seen it. After all, does a commodities trader in Wall Street have to see hog bellies and platinum bars? What's more, the Capras and Zanfardinos handled cash. Only cash. The money would be delivered to the storefront social clubs in suitcases and pillowcases. The Moustache Petes would count the tens and twenties, and then the Ernie Boys would be dispatched to begin the delivery. The heroin buyer would be asked for his car keys. Ernie Boy would take the car, and the buyer would be told to come back in three or four hours, or he would be told to go home and wait for a call. The call might come in an hour, or it might come the next day. The buyer would be told where to come to pick up his car keys. And, when he'd pick up his keys, he'd be told where his car was. There would be no mention of heroin. When the buyer reached his car, he'd drive it to a safe place and then open his trunk. And there the heroin would be, all neatly packed in plastic bags.

Pleasant Avenue's wholesalers had a reputation for prompt delivery and for dealing only high-quality heroin. They ran the Tiffany's of junk. If you were a Nicky Barnes or a Black Zack, if you paid your money, and if you were promised a delivery by the weekend, then that's what you got. If something ever went wrong with a package, the Moustache Petes on The Avenue would be asking a lot of questions, and they would keep on asking questions until they began to get correct answers.

Vinnie was paid well, about two to three hundred dollars per package, plus expenses. But, by the end of the week, he was usually broke. Ernie Boy's friend Vito would joke about it and say that Vinnie's problem was that he was "feeding his nose" too much.

"I like snorting coke myself, but don't you think you're going a little heavy. It ain't candy, Vinnie. You're going to make all those Spic bastards in Jersey rich selling you the stuff, and you're going to have a big fucking nose and no bread."

Vinnie would flick a thumbnail off his front tooth and tell Vito not to worry so much. "You're a fucking pig farmer, or else you'd know what it takes to be a good stickman. Don't you know that your nose and your prick are all hooked up inside. I'm in demand, you know, and I don't want to go around disappointing no broads."

"If you're so good with the chicks, Vin, how come you're not coming on stronger with Stella. She should be your old lady already. You know, with her you been sticking it in a lot of bread. Like maybe five million big ones."

"You think her old man's got that kind of bread?"

"I don't think, I know. Outside of maybe Capra and Armando, Nunzi is got more action going than anybody on The Avenue. He's connected all over. Last week, I moved three packages for him and another guy I know moved two. And one package I took over to Brooklyn, like four in the morning, had to be three kilos. I have two shotguns in the car, and I was driving down Delancey and over the bridge like fifteen miles an hour, checking the mirror and everything that moved in the street. That's how uptight I was. By the time I got to Brooklyn, I was so shitting in my pants that I called the big nigger that picks up for Boyd and told him to meet me, you know where? Right fucking in front of a police station. I'd rather be fucking busted

than drive a package like that into some nigger block in
Brownsville."

Vinnie and Stella had known each other since the first
grade and they were hitting it off much better than Vito or
anyone on The Avenue knew. By March, Stella *was* Vinnie's
old lady. "I had the lukewarms for your Vinnie when I was still
playing with dolls," Stella would later tell the old man.
   And, Stella had the same contempt for her father that Vinnie had for his. "You know what my Pop's idea of a good time
is? To go over to Orchard Beach. Orchard Beach! He could
have five yachts, and he rolls up his pants and goes wading
over at Orchard Beach.
   "And that candy store. You know I was twelve years old,
and we were still living in back of that candy store. And all
the guys from The Avenue were coming in there, three, four
in the morning and doing business with Pop practically in my
bed.
   "And you think you can get him to go anywhere? 'What's
in Vegas?' he says. The man is fifty-three years old and he's
never taken a vacation. Not one day."
   Both Vinnie and Stella were in a hurry to go places. They
went over to City Island and College Point a lot. Walking
along the marinas they dreamed of having their own big
yacht and seeing all the places that Stella read about in
magazines. Stella was big on magazines and brochures put
out by the airlines.
   Once on a Saturday night she got Vinnie to take her to
Aruba when he had to be back on The Avenue Monday morning to move a package. If Stella had the lukewarms for Vinnie, she had the hots for the world, the world way far away
from Pleasant Avenue—the world her father didn't want to
hear about.
   One Sunday Stella and Vinnie went to Port Jefferson on

Long Island to look at "real fancy boats." In the car on the way out, they began to talk about her father's business.

"I bet we could borrow a kilo from him, and he'd never know the difference," Stella said.

"What are you, crazy?"

"No, I mean it. He's funny. Sometimes he'll put a shipment away, my brother Dom says, and won't touch it for weeks. All he tells Dom is that he's got his reasons. Vinnie, you're always saying we could be rich if you could deal one load your way. Are you sure?"

"I got a nigger in Brooklyn that would give me half of what he makes on a key and he cuts heavy and bags it all the way to the street. If we could get him stuff on a Wednesday, say, by the next Monday, it could mean for us maybe forty, fifty thousand."

"Forty, fifty thousand."

"But, baby, how you going to just up and *borrow* that much stuff from your pop. That's heavy stuff. I know that a lot of the guys are skimming packages. Okay, maybe you can do an ounce or two a week that way. But you fool around too much and, zappo, Campopiano, or one of the boys from 116th, is going to be coming around looking for your neck."

Stella was sure they would have a chance. And, in their fashion, they waited a long time—three days.

Everybody in the family knew not to go near an upstairs closet in the house of Stella's elderly great-aunt out in Astoria.

"If he's got anything put away, it would be in that closet. For Pop, Aunt Carola's place is like a vault in the bank."

Stella was right about the closet. But, she was wrong about her Aunt Carola. Like Herbie Sperling's mother, Aunt Carola was a tough piece of work. And, she didn't buy Stella's story that she and Vinnie were in the neighborhood and just happened to stop by. As soon as they left, Aunt Carola was on the phone to Nunzi. Nunzi asked if Stella and her boyfriend had been to the closet, and Aunt Carola said, "I think so." And Nunzi went over to check.

That afternoon, when Nunzi's boys came to the old man's apartment looking for Vinnie, they wouldn't tell him what it was about. As soon as they left, the old man called a nephew who was able to get the phone number for Vinnie's apartment on East Eighty-first Street.

"What kind of trouble you in, Vinnie?"

"Nothing, Pops, nothing."

"Don't tell me nothing. Guys from 116th were here looking for you. Nunzi sent them looking for you."

"That fucking old lady. I got to go, Pop, I got to move out, fast."

Stella wanted to call her father. But, Vinnie said it would do no good. They left Vinnie's car in the street and rented one and drove all night to a motel in West Virginia.

A week later, Stella called her father.

Hysterically, she pleaded with him to let her come home. "It was very dumb, Pop, I know. I know. Please, please, please."

Nunzi spoke calmly. "What are you crying about? Sure you can come home. And, that boyfriend of yours, he can come home. I got coffins for both of you."

Vinnie called the old man. "You got to help me, Pop. I'm sorry. I'm sorry. Can you square it for me? I still got the kilo. I'll bring it back. I'll do whatever they say. Just square it for me. Square it for me. I was going to return it. We were just going to make what we could and then buy from ounce men and make up a kilo and return it. I swear it, Pop."

Several days later the old man called me. He said he'd had a sitdown with Nunzi. "Nunzi finally stopped talking about coffins, but that Stella bitch of his is going to be sent away someplace, and my Vinnie is marked lousy for life on The

Avenue. Nobody will ever lift a finger for him, not even for a straight job. He couldn't be a plumber's helper now. Nunzi put the word around. My kid's alive only because of people who know people in my wife's family.

"So all we've been talking about, David, what does it mean? I got my Vinnie back, and he lays in the bed and smokes one cigarette. And he smokes another cigarette. And he stares at the ceiling, and you think he says one word to his father? You think he learned something? I don't know.

"And I'm lucky. I can walk in the house and my kid is there. My friend Angelo, a good man, his kid was just DOA at Metropolitan Hospital. A sixteen-year-old kid and, just like that, dead from the needle.

"Angelo's kid is dead. Little Fonzo is dead. And, my Vinnie is lying in the bed, looking at the ceiling.

"You listening to me, David?"

6. City Hall Involvement

Vinnie was out of the heroin business. Nunzi had been told to lay off. And the old man had had the satisfaction of showing his son what a real father was. But everything else on The Avenue was still the same.

Capra, Zanfardino, Guarino were still out there dealing kilo-lots of heroin. The news of The Avenue was that Abbamonte had bought himself a big house near Frank Costello's place in Sands Point on Long Island.

The old man was incredulous. "David, can you imagine a fucking punk like Ernie Boy has the bread for Sands Point, and he's living down the road from Costello? Frank Costello, David!"

It all seemed unreal. The old man had given me information on the inner workings of the wholesale heroin business. I had checked out plates and cars and storefronts and had turned over everything I had to SIU. Other police and city officials knew what I had. And, nothing was happening.

There I was, going back and forth to the moribund Department of Investigation, handling bullshit cases of petty thievery, and chewing on my liver. And interior decorators and carpet salesmen out in Sands Point were nodding their heads and saying, "Yes, Mr. Abbamonte, no, Mr. Abbamonte. Tuesday, Mr. Abbamonte."

I was desperate and decided to try to arrange a meeting with the mayor, John Lindsay, thinking that in a face-to-face encounter I could persuade him of the horror on Pleasant Avenue. Some time back I had become well acquainted with one of Lindsay's principal aides, Jay Kriegel, and on the night of March 28, 1969, Jay accompanied me on a surveillance tour of Pleasant Avenue.

We drove to East Harlem in Kriegel's green MG-B convertible. As usual, the Cadillacs and the Continentals were double- and triple-parked on The Avenue outside the storefront heroin brokerages. In report after report, the SIU detectives said the cars were not there. And, night after night, there they were.

Kriegel was aghast. "If what you're saying about the heroin dealing is true, David, we'll have to get right on it." A Pleasant Avenue operation could not survive without the worst kind of corruption in the police ranks from the local precincts to the police commissioner's office.

Kriegel served as Lindsay's day-to-day liaison with Police Commissioner Howard Leary. And, since 1965, I had briefed him on corruption in the plainclothes gambling squad. I had also told him about my earlier meetings with the old man.

"Jay, this isn't the Bronx, this isn't Serpico telling us about a gambling pad. This is heroin, and this is cops selling guns to hoods. And what's the point of being in office for four years if you can't do something about an operation as ugly as Pleasant Avenue?"

Kriegel knew that I had been to Ruskin about Pleasant Avenue and had asked for a D of I investigation. And, he knew that Ruskin had said this couldn't be done. Kriegel knew that Ruskin had turned it over to Leary and that Leary had turned it over to SIU and that SIU was no longer even answering my phone calls. He knew how Renaghan and Tange had reacted, and he knew that Leuci had hinted to me that something was wrong at SIU.

He couldn't send me back to the department. I had been there. But, as we sat in his car, it became clear to me that he was not able to make a commitment to take immediate action. And he didn't want to know too much about cops selling heroin. Not then. Maybe sometime. But not then.

"Not now, David. You have to understand about priorities. John has a primary and an election to get through. If we can get reelected, I promise you that the police corruption matter will be given the highest priority."

I was furious. I wanted Kriegel and the mayor to use their power to find out what was going on in SIU and in East Harlem. I wanted action. And I didn't want to lose the confidence of the old man. Kriegel wasn't even willing to make one phone call. All I was getting was more bullshit. True, it was articulate, cultured bullshit, but it was bullshit. Essentially, Kriegel was saying that it made more sense, politically, for the mayor to live with narcotics corruption than to expose it. He made it clear that no action would be taken against Pleasant Avenue or SIU for at least seven months. Nothing could be done in Kriegel's view before the November election.

That March night, that ride through East Harlem with Kriegel would turn out to be an important one for me, for Kriegel, for Lindsay, and for the city of New York.

I realized then that I would have to blow the whistle on Kriegel, Lindsay, Leary—the whole fucking system—if I was to keep faith with the old man on Pleasant Avenue and if I was to truly do anything about high-level narcotics dealing and about corruption in the police department.

In that spring of 1969, Mayor John Lindsay, looking grim and earnest, went on television and said, "The war on narcotics must be as great a national commitment as was the war on poverty. . . ." And the man who wrote such things for the mayor, Jay Kriegel, would sit in a cold car with me and ask me to wait seven months to move against the city's major heroin dealing operations—operations run by the Mafia and by the Narcotics Division of the NYPD.

Jay confidently talked about priorities. "David, David, David . . ." Didn't I understand that t-h-e m-o-s-t i-m-p-o-r-t-a-n-t t-h-i-n-g was getting the mayor reelected? "That's the ball game, right now." Didn't I realize that if Lindsay was reelected he had every chance of making it to the White House? "The White House, David." And, didn't I know that Jay Kriegel would be as important in the Lindsay White House as Ted Sorensen was in the Kennedy White House? "What do you really want to do with your life, David?"

Kriegel and the young men around Lindsay were dedicated to their boss and truly believed that they would follow John V. Lindsay from City Hall to the White House. His face would be on postage stamps. Lindsay would be the thirty-eighth President of the United States. And Jay Kriegel, just seven or eight years out of Midwood High School, Brooklyn, would be in a limo riding back and forth between the White House and the good life of Fairfax County, Virginia. Kriegel could see Georgetown, the Mercedes-Benz showroom in Alexandria, the rolling red clay hills of Virginia, the poolside parties. . . .

But I was rocking the boat. Durk was the prick who could just ruin it all. Durk couldn't stop talking about the old man, the old man, the old man. SIU, SIU, SIU. If he could just get me to understand the dynamics of campaign strategy. What would Lindsay gain by pissing off the cops just when he needed them? Hadn't the teachers' strike and the garbage strike and the Civilian Review Board fight done enough to hurt the mayor? He couldn't be out front on this one. Not now. Didn't I understand what a police narcotics scandal would do? Lindsay needed the cops, he needed the ethnics. He didn't want to have the Patrolmen's Benevolent Association on his ass. And what was more important with the summer coming on? Corruption among some narcotics detectives, or keeping the lid on in Bed-Stuy and in Harlem and on the whole city?

Sophistry and cant, which had always been part of the scene, dominated the Lindsay City Hall. Cops were seen as lumbering brutes (with hands that could block the sun) who were pilfering apples off fruit stands since the beginning of time. A smart mayor didn't take them on. The cops could hurt you. Put medals on their shirts, and march in their parades, and rush to the hospital when they get shot or stabbed. And leave everything else to the police commissioner. And don't piss off the commissioner by asking too many tough questions.

A book called *Governing New York City* by two prominent Ivy League professors, Wallace Sayre and Herbert Kaufman, became the bible of the Lindsay administration. The book contains the following passage:

> However aggressively the [Police] Commissioner pursues the goal of police integrity by the use of special squads to investigate the force, by shake-ups and transfers of command, by swift suspensions and other forms of discipline, he accepts that police corruption is endemic to his organization, and that he is fortunate if he can prevent its reaching epidemic proportions. He lacks the resources to do more.

Two professors wrote that nonsense and a mayor and the mayor's men adopted it as gospel. For months after that March night with Kriegel, I hoped that somehow Kriegel would do something. But no initiative was forthcoming from City Hall, from the Department of Investigation, or from the police commissioner. Silence.

Mimeographed handouts continued to pour out of City Hall on what the administration was doing to crack down on heroin dealing. Kriegel and the other image-makers worked long and hard to make their boss look good. In the newspapers, Lindsay was putting the screws to Leary. The mayor ordered every man assigned to a narcotics unit to make at least four narcotics felony arrests a month. The mayor, the press releases said, was determined to drive dope dealers out of the city. It was a cruel hoax. The Lindsay edict produced arrests that rarely led to convictions.

In 1965, the year John V. Lindsay became mayor of New York City, there were about 350 heroin-related deaths. Four years later, the statistics in heroin-related deaths had more than tripled, to nearly 1,100 for 1969 alone. Excluded are killings resulting from disputes among heroin dealers and addicts. Pushers were picked up off street corners to meet the mayor's arrest quotas, but most were soon released without trial and back on the street. Month after month, the same low-level pushers were picked up, processed, and released. The arrest figures looked great, but hardly anyone was going to jail. Any fifteen-year-old kid could walk half a block in Brownsville and buy all the bags of heroin he wanted. Kids were dying from the stuff in alleys and backyards all over the city and by the time the medical examiners got there the bodies were often half-eaten by rats. Children in these neighborhoods saw this. Good cops, decent men in the precincts, sickened by this and by the talk and actions of the cynics and rip-off artists among them, left the force, and often the city. Some of the best men in the department left in 1969, 1970, and 1971 with broken hearts and often in fear, afraid to tell loving wives what they had seen and heard.

Swift action against Pleasant Avenue in 1969 by Lindsay and SIU and Tange, Renaghan, Walsh, and Leary would have saved hundreds of lives and police careers. It would have

done a lot to save the public-school system from ruin. It
would have taken thieving judges off the bench. And it would
have allowed people in the neighborhoods, like the old man
on Pleasant Avenue, to begin to believe in the rule of law. But
such things didn't have a high priority.

A few months after Lindsay's reelection, the *New York
Times* published a series of front-page articles containing
information on widespread corruption in the New York City
Police Department. These *Times* articles by David Burnham
produced such heat that the mayor was obliged to appoint
a commission to investigate the information in Burnham's
articles. The information had been given to Burnham and the
editors of the *New York Times* by several police officers,
including me.

At first, Lindsay appointed a commission made up of Po-
lice Commissioner Leary, Ruskin, two district attorneys, and
City Corporation Counsel Lee Rankin to investigate the
charges in Burnham's articles. But there was criticism that
Leary and the others were not independent enough, and
Lindsay was obliged to appoint a second commission.

The second commission, headed by Whitman Knapp, a
Wall Street lawyer, eventually found that Lindsay himself
could not "escape responsibility" for the corruption in his
administration, but the mayor was not called to testify. Manhattan District Attorney Frank Hogan considered pressing
perjury charges against that Jay Kriegel on the basis that
Kriegel had given contradictory testimony under oath to
the Knapp Commission. The Knapp Commission's power to
take testimony under oath had expired before Kriegel testified at the open session, so no such charges were ever
brought.

My relationship with Kriegel began in the summer of
1965. I was a cop in uniform doing a four-to-midnight tour
near Central Park. A crowd had gathered on a street corner

to listen to a sidewalk orator standing on a chair making some political remarks. It was in the finest Hyde Park tradition, but some people in the crowd didn't like what the speaker was saying and were trying to stop him. As the cop on the beat, I stepped in to calmly and firmly remind all concerned of the constitutional provision for free speech. The crowd quieted down, and the speaker continued.

As I walked farther down the block, twirling my nightstick, a man called after me. Accompanied by a young lady, the young man said he wanted to compliment me on what I had just done. The compliment was nice, and I thanked him for it. He began to ask thoughtful questions about police work, which I was happy to answer. The pleasant young fellow was Jay Kriegel. His date was the daughter of Thomas "Tommy the Cork" Corcoran.

Kriegel told me that he had just graduated from law school, had an offer to clerk for Justice Thurgood Marshall, and was working in the mayoral campaign of Congressman John V. Lindsay.

In the course of conversation, I must have asked Kriegel about where he had gone to college. He said Amherst. I said, "Oh, really? So did I" and introduced myself as Patrolman David B. Durk, Amherst, class of '57.

Kriegel was amazed that an Amherst man was walking a beat in a sweaty police uniform with a nightstick, a gun, and a pair of handcuffs. He and Miss Corcoran looked at each other blankly. As if I had to defend myself, I said, "What's wrong about an Amherst man being a cop?" I said some people were going into the Peace Corps to help change things, and I had become a cop with the same hope.

That evening I had the company of Kriegel and Miss Corcoran for nearly half my tour. They were good listeners, and I regaled them with the precinct war stories that patrolmen, young and old, like to tell. Kriegel asked for my telephone number and asked if he could call me.

A few days later he called and soon we began to spend a lot of time together talking about politics, crime, and police work. Kriegel was high on Lindsay and said that the hacks would no longer be running New York City if the young Republican Congressman were elected mayor.

Kriegel was eager to have my thoughts on anything that had to do with the police. By the end of summer, we began to write position papers on crime to be used by Lindsay in the campaign. When Lindsay got elected, Kriegel became a mayoral assistant with an office in City Hall. Through Kriegel I became part of Lindsay's far-flung and loosely knit kitchen cabinet. I had many suggestions for improving police procedures. Kriegel wrote my suggestions up in long memoranda to the mayor. Both Lindsay and his brother George were police buffs, and they had an idea that the answer to street crime was to saturate the neighborhoods with cops on motorcycles. This was bullshit. I told Kriegel we already had too many uniform cops in certain commands on patrol and that we should have more plainclothesmen and decoy cops assigned to catching muggers, rapists, burglars, car thieves, and the like. The scarecrow theory of blanketing the city with blue uniforms just didn't work.

What we needed wasn't more cops but changes in the attitudes and work habits of those we had. Cops needed more self-respect, and clearly something had to be done about the wiseguys and malingerers on the force.

I remembered the first time I turned out on patrol from a station house in Harlem. As soon as we left the block the station house was on, my partner, an older cop, said rather casually that he was going to the movies.

"What if we get a call?" I asked. "Won't the sergeant want to know where you are?"

He called back as he walked off: "Just tell him I heard

screams down the block and went to investigate. He'll understand."

In those days, many cops assigned to Harlem patrol duty spent their entire tours watching old John Wayne and Esther Williams movies from the balcony of the RKO Alhambra.

Morale was low in the department. Active, hardworking cops often got in trouble for their efforts. An active cop made the malingerers look bad.

Kriegel sat in my living room for hours at a time making detailed notes. And later he would sit in his basement office in City Hall until three or four o'clock in the morning, transforming these notes into memos for Lindsay.

Sadly, these Kriegel memos never brought about changes in the system. Kriegel used them to impress Lindsay, and Lindsay used them to impress Leary. But they were never acted upon.

Conditions in the department didn't improve. The cynics and the crooks on the force seemed to make all the rules and, as I would later tell the Knapp Commission, "Decent cops were told in a hundred ways every day to forget the law, don't make waves, and shut up."

Things got so bad that I asked Kriegel if the mayor would see a few good policemen so that they could tell him what it was like to work in the precincts and in the plainclothes squads. Kriegel said he would see what he could do. Then he called me to say that a meeting with the mayor had been arranged. A small number of cops agreed to accompany me to see the mayor. But, shortly before the meeting was to take place, it was canceled abruptly and without explanation. Kriegel was very nervous. He wanted to know how many people had known about the meeting, and he told me to make sure to forget about it.

This first attempt to discuss police corruption with the mayor took place in 1966, three years before I took Kriegel on that ride to Pleasant Avenue. So, over a period of four years, the mayor's office knew. Kriegel was told first about systematic payoffs to the police by bookmakers and numbers men, and about widespread malingering in the station houses and finally about police involvement in heroin dealing. Nothing was done about it. I never talked with Mayor John Lindsay until after the Knapp Commission hearings when he tried to shake my hand at the Police Academy and complimented me on the fine work I had done. He asked me if he could call me David, and he said that he had always admired me from afar.

7. A Good Year for Heroin

For New York City's heroin bosses, 1969 was a good year. Capra and Sperling and a number of the others had developed excellent overseas multi-kilo connections. They could buy directly from heroin labs in Marseilles or from heroin jobbers in Beirut, Tel Aviv, Paris, Frankfort, Amsterdam, and Montreal. Six or seven wholesalers on Pleasant Avenue were bringing in enough heroin to supply most of the major street dealers from Brooklyn to Detroit.

The vast black ghetto of central Brooklyn and the decaying Brownsville section were flooded with Pleasant Avenue heroin. Hundreds of thousands of three-dollar bags, five-dollar bags, ten-dollar bags, and fifty-dollar spoons of heroin were offered for sale every day. Heroin was sold from baby carriages, from shopping bags, from junked cars, from the pushcarts of sidewalk vegetable peddlers, in bar after bar, in alleys, tenement stairwells, and junior-high-school classrooms.

A cop on patrol, a street cleaner, a welfare worker, or a Kriegel or Lindsay out campaigning could see the worst of the addicts sleeping on sidewalks or slumped over nodding out against tenement walls. They would be stretched out in pools of vomit. Nearby preschool children would be playing with a ball or a rope or a tricycle. And, darting back and forth, from bar to bar, from apartment building to apartment building, "doing business," were the pushers making their drops and picking up cash for heroin that would be delivered "later tonight, man, when my man brings the shit from Harlem. He's

The corner: Pleasant Avenue and 117th Street. Early in the day it was the center of bookmaking, numbers, and loan sharking in East Harlem. In the afternoon the heroin dealers arrived and often conducted business until dawn. Orders to pick up and deliver millions of dollars' worth of heroin were relayed in code from the twin phone booths on the corner.

up there with the Italians, you dig, he's bringing dynamite, greaseball dy-na-mite."

The principal heroin dealer in Bedford-Stuyvesant, Rufus Boyd, and his counterpart in Brownsville, a black man who called himself Big Dutch Schultz, were well known to the precinct cops and to just about everybody in the neighborhoods. Everyone knew they were heroin dealers, but they walked the streets of Brooklyn with an air of respectability and with the bearing of successful businessmen. They had been around for years. Most people, cops among them, came to believe they could never be touched.

Big Dutch even managed to develop a reputation for charity and benevolence. He took care of his people. A girl addict who was pregnant and sick and couldn't hustle money and couldn't make it to the street to buy heroin would be supplied with the stuff until the baby came. Big Dutch would make it his business to know about hardship cases. He knew the neighborhood, he knew his people, and he was one of the few dealers willing to carry some addicts on credit.

The frenetic scurrying about of the heroin dealers and addicts in Brownsville gave a kind of perverse vitality to the decaying neighborhood. There was the stink of vomit and urine and garbage in the streets and the incessant barking of packs of stray dogs. But there was also a kind of gold-rush excitement. Few outside the neighborhood knew it, but there was a lot of money to be made in Brownsville. Fast money. The merchants on Pitkin Avenue knew it, the cops in the 73rd Precinct knew it, the poverty pimps who worked for Lindsay knew it, and the Italian bosses who were close to the heroin action on black streets knew it.

Both blacks and whites in Brownsville talked of "getting nigger rich." And, indeed, heroin trafficking created a kind of prosperity amid the worst kind of poverty. Teams of plainclothes cops in '57 Chevys, many from outside the district, worked overtime searching out addicts and pushers to score. Much in the manner of pirates at sea, they would jump two or three blacks in a doorway, take whatever money or heroin or jewelry they could find and rush off to their next rip-off. It all made for great conversation later at the station house or the local watering hole. Police officers with wives and children in the suburbs would leave their homes day after day. They'd wave to their kids from their driveways, wish them luck in Little League games, and go off to the city for another night of heroin plundering.

White merchants, the proprietors of little Mom-and-Pop stores on Pitkin Avenue, learned to stock glassine envelopes and to price them at three and four times their worth. They

sold these envelopes in the tens of thousands to heroin dealers, who used them to package heroin. In a year of good
business, such a shopkeeper could sell his old jalopy, buy a
new Dodge, and think about leaving the old walk-up apartment in East Flatbush and "just maybe" buying a nice house
in Queens or near their children on Long Island.

"If the shvartzers didn't buy from me, they'd buy from
somebody else. So what's the difference?" It was legal. It
was also legal for druggists to sell eyedroppers and quinine
and three or four other items used by dealers to package
junk or by addicts to shoot-up. During a gold rush, you don't
ask questions.

People who did got nowhere. A salesman who sold paper
products wholesale told me his company was selling huge
amounts of glassine envelopes to a small number of dealers
in Bed-Stuy and Brownsville. "There suddenly can't be so
many stamp collectors in Brooklyn, right? Something maybe
ain't so kosher. Something must be a lot wrong." There was
something a lot wrong and I went to Captain Tange and SIU
with the information and suggested an investigation. I was
sure that important information could be gained about heroin operations by putting the stores selling the envelopes
under surveillance. Tange wasn't interested. "We don't work
that way, Durk. We work from the bottom up."

The mayor's speech writers turned out nifty pieces on the
scourge of heroin, and the department made "show" arrests,
but, in truth, cynicism and sham prevailed. Honest men in the
department were kept away from the mayor and from any
chance of putting Pleasant Avenue and SIU and all the wiseguys in the precinct clubs out of business.

Lindsay and Leary asked young officers just out of the
Police Academy to undertake perilous undercover assign-
ments just to make bullshit "show" collars of low-level dealers. They asked young, earnest guys in their early twenties
to risk their lives in alleyways, just to get a few grains of

heroin off the street, enough for a press release. At the same time, the mayor wouldn't risk his *political* life and his chance at the White House by going against either the multi-kilo dealers on Pleasant Avenue or the heroin-scoring cops in SIU.

In fairness, Lindsay shouldn't take all the weight for what happened in New York City during the years of unchecked heroin dealing and police corruption. He shares the responsibility with others—with "distinguished others" of the bench and of the bar. It was all too clear from the flow of narcotics cases through the courts in the 1960s and from the transcripts that the "big fix" was in. Too many narcotics felony cases were disposed of without indictments, trials, or conviction. Too many known dealers, who *were* arrested again and again were released without serving time even after conviction.

One former assistant district attorney in Frank Hogan's prestigious office put it plainly: "The odor would have offended a skunk. A lot of judges knew that the gambling and narcotics cases were bullshit, but there they sat in their black robes, just processing corrupt cases through, clearing their calendars before lunch, and then taking off for the golf courses."

After the Knapp Commission documented a pattern of widespread police corruption in New York, and after SIU detectives began to be indicted for their past crimes, one prominent jurist confided to an intimate that he was much relieved by the mass indictments of SIU detectives.

"Now I can sleep nights. Thank God. These bastards from SIU have been coming before me day after day for years and perjuring themselves, and I've done nothing about it."

8. The Stalemate Continues

I didn't want the old man to lose heart. I'd call him up and ask about Vinnie.

"What can I tell you, David? Most of the time he stays in his room with the door closed. He don't put pants on, nothing. If I get him to say something to his father, he says his life is finished.

"He's driving us both crazy. My wife, you should see her. She's up all night walking the floor with cramps and the doctor, already, gave her belladonna and pills and prescriptions and prescriptions. She can't even catch her breath walking the stairs. A women who walked stairs all her life, David. It's just no good.

"A little cunt like Nunzi's Stella and my asshole kid, Vinnie, and all the punks on The Avenue—they want it all. Everything or nothing. Vinnie all the time says he wants to be a somebody. Right? And a somebody by him isn't a shmuck like me who sits eight hours by a Linotype machine. A somebody is an Ernie Boy with a house like Costello's got. A somebody is a guy like Capra who goes out bouncing in his Thunderbird bringing in five, ten, who-the-hell-knows-how-many kilos a week.

"This fucking kid of mine. You know it was his birthday last Friday. Hallelujah, he was eighteen years old. Eighteen, should be in school, taking girls to Roseland, and what's in his head? Ripping off Nunzi for a kilo. Fancy apartments. Niggers who can make him a millionaire.

"You have children today, and all they do is bleed you. My friend Angelo, I told you, his kid—he should rest in peace— died from the needle. And Angelo, now he don't even play dominoes. And Angelo loved dominoes. He was a good player. And my wife . . ." The old man mumbled something in Italian. "My wife and me, we lay in bed and don't even talk."

I asked the old man if he and his wife would come to my place one night for dinner.

"You're kidding me, David. My wife? Evelina don't even know about you. How could I tell her about you? She'd kill me. You think she wants me talking about The Avenue. Nobody talks about The Avenue."

"All right, I'll tell you what. Why don't you come to my place straight from work. I'll go out and get some fresh Genoa salami, real good stuff, some mozzarella, and I've got sausages. I'll make some linguini, we'll have wine. You're coming? Right?"

"You really mean it, David? You want me to come to your place?"

"Yes. Yes."

"All right, I'll come. I know what I'll do. I'll tell Evelina I'm going to Angelo's. But, listen to me, David, don't make soup. Evelina made a pot of busecca. It's delicious. You ever have busecca? It's tripe soup with bacon and pinto beans, potatoes, carrots. My mother used to make busecca. But, Evelina makes it better.

"It's the pot. She makes it in a special pot her grandmother brought from Sicily. She's got that pot ever since we're married and, you know what, that pot's never been scrubbed. That's the secret. Brillo has never touched that pot. If you want good busecca you need a pot like that."

I listened, and I was glad that I had never told the old man about my meeting with Kriegel. The old man knew enough shame.

The old man was coming for dinner so I left the Department of Investigation a little early and went home to shop and cook. Before jumping in the shower, I put the sauce for the linguini on the stove to simmer. After showering and shaving, I dressed and went downstairs to shop.

It was five o'clock, rush hour in New York, as I strode along Seventy-second Street and headed for Zabar's. Salvador Dali has said that the three most marvelous places in the world are Paris, Rome, and Bonwit Teller's. I would have to add Zabar's. I had the usual shopper's anxieties. I was sure Zabar's and the wine store would be loaded with people and that it would take twenty minutes in each store for me to get waited on. The old man was coming at seven so I was rushing along not waiting for lights and skipping around baby carriages, kids on skate boards, and around an old lady with rolled stockings and an apron.

At the corner of Seventy-second and Columbus, I heard a woman screaming, hysterically. I saw a car double-parked near the Ruxton Hotel. There was a crowd around the car and, although my view was obstructed, the screams seemed to come from the car or near it.

I ran over. The hysterical woman was an attractive girl in her twenties, white, who was resisting four men, all blacks, who were trying to get her into the car.

As I pushed through the crowd, I saw the girl was bleeding from the nose and a cut near her eye. I pulled out my shield, identified myself, and ordered the four men to release the girl.

"What the fuck is wrong with you people?" I screamed. The men ignored me and continued pummeling the girl. She was yelling, "They're going to kill me. They're going to kill me." I screamed at the guys, warning them to let her go, but it was like I wasn't there. It was rush hour in New York. Lots of people were around. I was a cop and had identified myself. But the beating went on. I was witnessing an assault in progress. I was trying to stop it and couldn't.

I grabbed hold of the girl and tried wrestling her away from her abductors.

One of the guys said, "Listen, pig, if you are a pig, this here girl is my wife, and this is family business. You hear me, man. You're butting your nose in only because I'm black and she's white."

"I don't care what color anybody is, just lay off, right now, you hear me, pal."

More blacks, unsavory-looking guys, started to gather around. "Hey, listen," one guy said to the crowd, "this here's just one honky pig, what's one pig, let's take him."

They moved toward me. I drew my gun. Instantly I had credibility. Even people conducting family business generally don't want to be shot. The guys let go of the girl, and the crowd was suddenly silent. No one was doing any more mouthing off, but I didn't know how long I could control the situation.

Finally, I heard the sweet sound of sirens. The troops arrived in several sector cars. A captain was in command.

I'll never forget the florid-faced captain's words. "Hey, what you got, kid?" the captain asked, peering at me and my shield number.

I tried to catch my breath so that I could reply. "Assault, captain, possible kidnapping."

The captain frowned. He looked at the girl and the four blacks who were all costumed in flashy electric-colored jump suits.

The captain looked annoyed. "Kid, don't you know what

you got here? These here are pimps and the female is a pros. What are you getting involved for? Why bother with these people? What they do with each other, kid, is their business."

I was out of breath. I was also scared. It all happened so fast. It was just like the first time I responded to a burglary-in-progress call and had to chase a fleeing man across a rooftop in the dark and was shot at. And here was this sonofabitch hairbag captain telling me that this was a bullshit collar. A throw-out.

"Listen, captain, I know she's a pros. So what? They were beating the hell out of her. They were dragging her off to a car. Just because she's a pros—does that mean she's not entitled to help from a cop when she's got real trouble?"

I asked the girl if she would press charges. I could see the fear in her face. Quietly she said, "No." The captain didn't let me ask her again or take her aside. "Get the hell out of here. All of you," he barked.

The girl, still bleeding from the nose and the cut near her eye, and the four dudes all got into the car, a bright yellow Caddie, and drove off toward Central Park.

The captain and his driver and the others from the precinct got back into their radio cars and drove off.

I walked on to Zabar's and to the wine store and then home.

The old man, my wife and daughters, were waiting in the dining room.

"Hello, Daddy. Look what your friend brought." There was the Sicilian artifact—the busecca pot that hadn't been scoured in twenty years—and under the wax paper was what must have been at least a gallon of tripe soup.

"It looks great," I said. I rushed to the kitchen and shouted back: "And wait till you taste the linguini. You smell the sauce?"

After dinner, we had coffee in the living room and I asked the old man if he'd like a spritzer.

"What's a spritzer, David?"

"It's terrific. You'll like it. Seltzer straight from the truck and white wine. After a spritzer, you'll be ready for another plate of linguini."

The old man laughed. "All right. Make me a spritzer."

I got up to get glasses and ice, and the old man followed me into the kitchen.

"David, maybe Evelina's home from bingo already. I don't want her to worry. Maybe I should call and tell her I'm just leaving Angelo and I'll be home soon."

He looked at his watch nervously. And he also looked at the clock on the wall. I showed him where the kitchen phone was and he dialed.

"Vinnie, is that you? Is Mama home from playing bingo yet? No? Where she go? Holy Rosary or Lady of Carmel? What? You're telling me your mother goes out and you don't even ask her where she's going? To a father you don't talk, and now also to a mother you don't talk?" The old man got angry and began shouting in Italian.

When he hung up the phone, the old man continued to mutter to himself. I asked him to come back into the living room.

He sat down slowly on the couch and turned to my wife. "David told you about my Vinnie?"

Arlene nodded. "A little bit."

"He lives in our house, that's about it. He doesn't talk to Evelina. He doesn't talk to me. I showed him what a father is. Right? And you think it means anything to him? He can't go on The Avenue anymore. So, he makes up his mind. The hell with everything—me, his mother, going back to school, learning something, getting a job. He's a smart boy. What does he do? The television he watches. Day and night. When the time comes, they'll have to put a television next to the casket to get him to come to my funeral.

"He's lucky I don't strangle him. A lousy indoor antenna we got. You can't see anything anyhow, and he sits all day and watches television. The worst crap is on and he watches. It could be two o'clock in the morning, and God forbid you want to turn the damn thing off. He won't let you, you know.

"It hurts me to say it. But, it's true. It's true, David. The sitdown. What I did. What you tried to do. Everything. It meant nothing. Not to that kid.

"If I had any sense, I'd get the hell away from The Avenue altogether. My kid, anybody's kid, he goes on The Avenue, he meets up with a *gavon* like Ernie Boy and that's it. He's finished. No more school. No more do you talk to a father. That's it.

"Angelo's brother, he's in my union. He moved to Rockaway. He tells me I'm crazy not to go to the union and get myself a loan to buy me a coop where he lives. You got the water there and the boardwalk. But it's an hour on the subway, David, and a bus ride. I'm sixty-three years old. And all Evelina's friends? Where are they? Here. And how can she leave bingo at Holy Rosary? And leave her sister who can't afford a Rockaway?"

The old man reached for the spritzer and gulped it down.

"I don't know," he said, pulling himself up from the couch.

"Let me go. It's crazy. I know I should get out. I should get my rotten kid out, far away from The Avenue. But, how? Where? I don't know. I got a Vinnie, David, I got a Vinnie."

The old man left, and I was very tired. I went to bed and fell asleep thinking about SIU's lack of interest in the old man's narcotics information, and about the precinct captain on Seventy-second Street, who told me I didn't know my job because I went to the aid of a screaming woman being dragged off by four men.

9. A Cop Speaks Out

The police department kept most of its records in an old eight-story building at 400 Broome Street in lower Manhattan. Before the department took it over, the building was a candy factory. A dumpy place, it was designed to hold cauldrons of steaming fudge and marshmallow, not people.

One of the joys of the place was getting from floor to floor. Hundreds of cops were in and out of the building all day, yet there was no passenger elevator. The Bureau of Criminal Identification had its huge files on known criminals on the fifth floor of 400 Broome. If a cop wanted to go through the BCI files, he had either to climb five flights of stairs or take his chances in an incredibly slow, undependable freight elevator.

During the summer of 1969, I went through the BCI files to try to learn as much as I could about Ernie Boy and Gigi and Nunzi and other mob figures of East Harlem. I used the files to introduce myself to the world of all the Funzis and, more specifically, to find out who owned the Cadillacs and Lincolns outside the storefronts on Pleasant Avenue.

In theory, you didn't have to go to 400 Broome to get information out of BCI. You could call and have one of the BCI cops check the files for you. But, as I told Inspector Lane, along with other detectives who didn't trust the system, I preferred to pull the files myself. There was too much talk in the department about BCI cops selling cases. It was all too

Heroin bosses. Gigi Inglese, second from left, and Gennaro (Jerry) Zanfardino, fourth from left, surveying The Avenue from the corner of 117th Street. Day after day, the same men would be on the same street corner overseeing the movement of hundreds of pounds of heroin. Note the lookout on the corner.

easy for a corrupt cop on clerical duty in BCI to function as a "lookout" for mob guys, to warn them whenever a detective or a headquarters boss called for information in their folders. It was a sad fact of life in the department that detectives spent precious hours going back and forth to BCI, hand-checking files rather than getting their information by telephone.

A detective worth his salt just wouldn't risk talking to a BCI clerical guy or to any cop he didn't know about an active organized crime investigation. To say the least, the department's record for safeguarding confidential information was a poor one. In case after case, targets of investigations would somehow learn that the heat was on, or that some cop was asking questions about them. One careless call to BCI or to the wrong clerical man in a precinct or at headquarters could burn months of investigative work and could also jeopardize the lives of witnesses and informants. Detectives learned the hard way to go through the files themselves. This slowed investigations, but, unfortunately, it was the only sure way to protect your cases and your informants.

The old man had told me to be careful. He knew with certainty that one cop was selling guns on The Avenue. If this was true, it was more than likely that this bastard and others were also selling information.

On one trip to 400 Broome, I got lucky. While waiting for the freight elevator, I met a cop I knew, an undercover detective who was assigned to SIU. Let's call him "Ray." Ray had a reputation for knowing his way around in the street and in the department.

Ray and I were not close friends. But we'd spent some time together in courthouse hallways while we were both waiting to testify in trials.

Detectives don't normally confide in one another unless they have worked together closely as partners or as members of the same squad. But Ray, for some reason, was quite open with me. Perhaps he felt close to me because of an incident that happened earlier. The summer before, in trying to control a large crowd of rioting antipoverty demonstrators, Ray was one of hundreds of cops rushed to City Hall plaza and badly beaten in the melee that followed. Ray knew I'd investigated the incident later for the D of I and found that the well-orchestrated "riot" was part of a plan by neighborhood hustlers to shake down the city.* I made a case against

---

*The hustlers were getting kickbacks from kids employed in Neighborhood Youth Corps summer jobs. The riot was organized to get the summer job program expanded. More summer jobs meant more rip-offs for the hustlers who controlled the Youth Corps payroll.

one of the organizers of the City Hall riot, and I think Ray may have been grateful to me for evening the score for him.

Ray was the perfect guy to talk to about SIU and the information the old man had given me about Pleasant Avenue. I told him I'd been given information on what might be very high-level heroin dealing. I took out my Pleasant Avenue diagrams and charts and began reading off the mobsters the old man said controlled the East Harlem heroin business.

Ray was startled when I read off the name Armando. He said the department had information that a man named Armando was the boss of bosses in New York's heroin trafficking. We went over every name on my list. Ray knew many of the Funzis, and his keen interest in the old man's information raised my spirits.

Ray and I got together a number of times after our chance meeting at 400 Broome. While talking one day, Ray suggested we have lunch at a restaurant in Chinatown. "They have a special noodle in this place, Dave, that's good for diarrhea and I've got the runs."

At lunch, Ray shocked me. He told me he wanted to get out of SIU and asked me if I could help him get reassigned.

"Can you get me into the D of I, Dave?"

"I don't know. Why do you want to leave SIU?"

"Things are really bad in SIU, David. The whole thing is really a mess, and it's going to blow wide open. I've got to get out. If I could work with you in the D of I, it would be good for me."

As Ray began to level with me, I remembered how Bob Leuci had come up to me after my first visit to SIU. I remembered Leuci's words: "Durk, don't put your heart into this one. Don't put your heart into this one."

"Something is really bothering you, Ray," I said. "Give it to me straight."

Ray didn't hesitate. He told me straight out that he and his partner had been approached by another detective in SIU to sell a heroin case. Ray said that he was convinced that SIU was full of bad cops and that he was afraid of them.

I asked him for all the specifics he could give me. Ray said he had been approached only once to take part in the selling of a case, but other detectives in SIU spoke openly he said, about scoring heroin money. He claimed some SIU detectives were getting from five thousand dollars to fifty thousand dollars per case to perjure themselves before grand juries and in trials. In addition, he knew major heroin dealers were paying SIU detectives fifty thousand to a hundred thousand for information on police wiretaps.

Ray gave me the names of a half-dozen SIU detectives he believed were scoring heroin money regularly.

I asked him if Captain Tange knew what was going on. Ray said he didn't think so. And he said he liked Tange and had no reason to question his integrity. He said he thought the whole mess was going to blow up because certain federal narcotics agents knew what corrupt cops in SIU were doing.

I was stunned.

I asked Ray to go with me to the office of the U.S. attorney in Manhattan. Ray agreed to go. He met with Robert Morvillo, chief of the criminal division, and Gary Naftalas, an assistant U.S. attorney. Ray told them the same story that he told me. So far as I know, the U.S. attorney's office did nothing with this information.

After his visit to the U.S. attorney's office, Ray was no longer eager to talk to me or anyone else about corruption in SIU. I talked with Paul Curran, then counsel for the New York State Investigations Commission. Curran said he was keenly interested in ferreting out corruption in narcotics law enforcement. I suggested to Curran that the SIC take testimony in secret from Ray and other detectives assigned to SIU.

Ray and other detectives were called in to testify. This secret testimony was important later on in federal and departmental investigations of corruption in SIU and the Narcotics Division.

Ray was not happy with me for having mentioned his name to Curran. "What the hell are you doing, David? How can I work with these guys in SIU, if you're going around town telling people that I'm an honest cop?"

On August 6, 1969, I was promoted to the rank of sergeant. I assumed that this would mean that I would become a sergeant of detectives in the Department of Investigation. This however, was not to be the case. The police command took me out of detective work and put me back in uniform to man the desk in the 34th Precinct station house in the Washington Heights section of upper Manhattan. I was put in charge of the precinct blotter, the precinct diary, and the precinct arrest records.

I was not particularly happy with my new assignment, and I asked Commissioner Ruskin if he could do something to keep me in detective work. Ruskin said he'd talk to Leary about keeping me in the D of I squad. There was another commissioner-to-commissioner conference on Durk. Ruskin told Leary he liked my work in the D of I and he'd like me to continue in the squad in my new rank. Such commissioner-to-commissioner requests were usually honored. This one was not. Leary said he wanted me in uniform, not in detective work.

I might still be behind the desk in the 34th Precinct if it had not been for the intervention of Henry Ruth, who was then director of the National Institute of Law Enforcement and Criminal Justice in Washington.

Ruth asked me to become a visiting fellow at the Institute and somehow managed to get Leary to give me a one-year leave to study new ways of attracting young men and women to police careers.

A grant went along with my appointment as visiting fellow

and made it possible for me to travel to college campuses and to talk to undergraduates about considering careers in police agencies. My message to the undergraduates was simple and direct: "If you really want to change things, become a cop."

I was Exhibit A: "The Amherst guy who became a cop." *Life* magazine did a spread on my college visits, and soon I had a long list of juniors and seniors from prestigious schools who wanted to do what I did.

Ruth had wanted me to visit the colleges to "test the waters." He wanted to see if there was enough interest on campus to fund later on a formal program in police recruiting. But, the harvest was immediate in practical terms. I brought back names of college seniors who were ready to go to work as policemen as soon as they graduated.

Ruth and I were excited about the possibilities. Too often, a police department is an inbred club, drawing new recruits from essentially the same population groups it has always drawn from. Departments need "new blood." Recruits from the colleges would bring with them new ideas and new expectations about police work.

I was extremely pleased by the widespread interest in police work that I found among college students. Bosses in the New York City Police Department weren't so pleased. I came back from one college trip and went down to police headquarters to report on my recruiting efforts. I remember the response of one deputy inspector in personnel.

"Durk, why do we want all those college kids coming here looking for jobs? They will only be troublemakers."

Many of the students I talked with on the campuses found jobs in police work, but not one found a job in New York City.

While working as a visiting fellow at the Institute, I was still a cop and, when I wasn't away from the city, I had a number of opportunities to make use of my badge and gun. One Sunday afternoon, I was looking out the window of my apartment in the West Seventies, just off Central Park. A young man in the street was going from parked car to parked car, looking into the windows. I watched the guy for a minute or so and then decided I had better go down to the street.

I was in the street only a few minutes when this character breaks the side window of a car, reaches in, takes out a Sony tape deck, and starts to make off with it. I'd seen enough. I made for the guy and stopped him on the sidewalk.

"Hi-ho, guess what?" I said. I identified myself and told him he was under arrest.

The young man responded to my greeting by pulling out a long knife from under his shirt. I pulled out my off-duty, snub-nosed revolver and placed it somewhere near his head. The young man's mood changed instantly. He became almost friendly and lost interest in his knife and his newly acquired tape deck.

"Look, it's a real good machine," he said. "Why don't you take it?"

"Listen, pal," I said. "This is for real."

The young man looked at me quizzically, with more than a touch of indignation in his eyes.

"If you're a cop," he observed, "where's your squad car? Where's your partner?"

I told the young man I was off duty.

"You're off duty?" He was infuriated. "If you're off duty, why the fuck are you looking to lock me up?"

I was tired of answering questions. I put the cuffs on him and commandeered a cab to take him to the nearest station house. In the cab, he asked if I wouldn't mind stopping in Central Park to tell his girl friend that he would be delayed. I told him I would be happy to oblige. "It's part of the service."

At the station house, I walked my prisoner to the desk. The desk officer on duty asked the usual question: "Whatcha got, kid?" I turned over the knife and the tape deck and offered a brief description of the crime.

It was just before a shift change at the station house, and I could tell that the desk officer was annoyed by having to process yet another arrest. Here I was, not assigned to that precinct, off duty, and I was making work for cops near the end of their shift. The desk officer was no less displeased with the arrest than was my prisoner. He frowned and mumbled to himself.

I tried to be diplomatic. After all, I didn't want this desk officer to find a way to cut this guy loose.

"Look, I'm really sorry," I said. "I really don't want to break your chops. But there was this huge crowd around. [I lied] Right in my own neighborhood. They knew I was a cop, and I couldn't avoid taking this guy in."

My mock apology worked. The arrest stuck. The young man pleaded guilty and was sentenced to ninety days. One of the reasons the arrest stuck was that I had a witness. A member of the state legislature, Richard Gottfried, was in the street at the time, saw the whole thing, and accompanied me to the station house.

The next day, I wasn't so lucky. I spotted another young fellow breaking into a vehicle. This time it was a plumber's truck, and the young man was making off with the plumber's tools. I grabbed the guy and, just as I was cuffing him, the plumber returned to his truck. "What are these tools worth?" I asked him.

"Two, maybe, three thousand dollars," he said.

I told him that it was lucky he'd come back to his truck just when he did. "This way I don't have to go looking for you to appear as a witness against this guy."

The plumber shook his head. "I'm not interested in going to no court."

I was incredulous. "You mean to tell me that this guy was ready to steal a couple thousand dollars' worth of your tools and you're not interested in seeing to it that he's put away?"

The plumber looked at me blankly.

"Listen, I could serve a subpoena on you, and you'd have to go to court," I told him.

"You can take your subpoena and shove it up your ass."

There was silence for a long moment. Then the expression on the plumber's face softened. "Listen, officer, I really appreciate what you did."

He reached into his pocket, took out a ten-dollar bill, and offered it to me.

"Why don't you take this, officer, and buy yourself a bottle?"

That was enough. I took off the cuffs and the perpetrator, the victim, and the cop went their separate ways.

10. Ripping Off the FHA

At eighteen, Vinnie was a burned-out, failed hustler. When he was working for Nunzi, he could walk into Leighton's and buy four suits and six pairs of shoes at one time and pay cash. Now, he had to ask his father for money to get a haircut.

While moving packages, he had a Thunderbird, his own apartment, girls, clothes, and, if he wasn't part of a night's action at the Tambourine, he was bouncing in the Village or running around with Cuban chicks in Jersey. Now, he found himself sitting on a folding chair in the walk-up apartment he hated on Pleasant Avenue, arguing with his mother over whether to watch Mike Douglas or the four-thirty movie on television.

Vinnie was in deep depression and shock. He still wasn't really sure that Nunzi would let him live. Maybe the sitdown was a stall. Maybe they'd still find him in a dump on Zarega Avenue or mutilated in a lake on Staten Island.

Vinnie was scared, angry, and alone. There was no Stella, no phone calls, no action, no money for cocaine or Valium or even pot. His father pestered him about things he didn't want to hear about. And his mother was dull. All he could do was wait, and he didn't know what he was waiting for.

By midsummer, Vinnie had had it with the apartment. He went down on The Avenue. Nobody would talk to him. But there were no hassles, no evil-eye looks, and over on First

Avenue a young numbers runner, Joe Farts, had a big hello for him. Vinnie figured that things couldn't be too bad if a guy like Joe Farts, who knew his way around, was friendly to him on the street.

Vinnie and Joe Farts went into Patsy's for a calzone. There was no talk of Nunzi or Vinnie's problem, but Vinnie was sure Joe Farts knew all about it. The whole neighborhood knew. And, Vinnie was sure that Sperling and the Jewish dealers down on Seventh Avenue knew. If he was marked lousy in the junk business on Pleasant, then he was marked lousy in the junk business, period.

Joe Farts was a little wearing to be with, but in Vinnie's predicament, company was company. Farts punctuated his talk with a variety of burps, gastric gurglings, and grimaces born of cramps. He was a Dantesque character, afflicted with what appeared to be lifelong indigestion. Farts's dyspeptic display could be unnerving, but people on The Avenue were used to it, just as they were used to Ernie Boy's brother-in-law, Johnny Echoes Campopiano, saying everything twice.

Without referring directly to Vinnie's problem, Joe Farts said it was no good for a guy like Vinnie to lay around.

"The Avenue ain't the world, Vin. You gotta think big. How about Brooklyn? I hear talk Brooklyn is wide open. There's lots of Brooklyn The Avenue got nothing to do with. Things ain't so good for you on The Avenue. So get your ass over to Brooklyn. You could make a connect with a sharp nigger or a Spic over there, or maybe get some Gallo action. You think Kid Blast gives a shit about The Avenue. They're doing their own thing."

"I hear Gallo's people are so tight with the spades they're trying to put a nigger maître d' into Callucci's."

"You got a regular United Nations in Callucci's. That's no Moustache Pete place anymore. They got everybody in there but gypsies."

Farts finished off his calzone and began massaging his belly with both palms. "Listen, Vin, me and Bath Beach got to take a pillowcase* over to Jewish Sam in Brooklyn tonight. Why don't you ride out with us, and we'll hit Luger's for supper and Bamonte's later on. Meet a few people."

Vinnie had once delivered a package for Nunzi to a guy in Bamonte's. It was a big sitdown place. And, Luger's was the biggest sitdown place in Brooklyn.

"Joey, why didn't I talk to you way before this? You got the wheels or Bath Beach got the wheels?"

"I got the wheels, Vin. I'll pick you up downstairs by your place."

Joe Farts talked all the way over to Brooklyn.

"Vin, they got action over in Williamsburg that you never heard of. I'm telling you. You know Bath Beach's cousin? The one that ain't right in the head. His mother would have been happy if he ended up a zookeeper. And he's working for Jewish Sam pulling down eight, nine big ones a week. This is a guy couldn't get himself laid in a whorehouse. That's the kind of action Jewish Sam has got. And I'm telling you it's brand-new action. Bread, bread, bread, and no heat. And nobody from The Avenue telling you you can't deal with this fucking guy or that fucking guy. When we're sitting in Luger's with Sam's people, do me a favor, just don't fall asleep. Keep your fucking ears open. You get close to Sam and, you'll see, The Avenue won't mean shit to you. Fuck The Avenue."

Jewish Sam was seated at a corner table near the back entrance to Luger's. Tommy Fantone was with him and there were some of Bummy Landsman's hoods from East Flatbush.

*The bookkeeping records of numbers operations were often transported around the city in pillowcases.

Joe Farts did the introductions. "This here is Vinnie. He's got a headache up on The Avenue. He fucked up real bad. But, he's a worker, Sam, and if you kick 'im in the balls every once in a while, he'll work out nice. Likes his nose too much and he's always sticking it in the wrong cunt, but that doesn't make him a bad person."

Jewish Sam leaned over the table as if he was going to shake Vinnie's hand, but instead he reached over to feel the material of Vinnie's maroon-and-black-checked sports coat.

"You got that in Maxi's, kid?"

"No, I get all my stuff in Leighton's."

"Leighton's? I wouldn't buy my draws in Leighton's."

"What's wrong with Leighton's?"

"Leighton's, Field Brothers, they're all buying novelty cloth from Honk Kong, Korea. . . . It's garbage. By Maxi's you get tailoring, and you get goods that'll wear like iron. What you got now is going to have holes in the crotch in two, three weeks. You got it reinforced? You should get it reinforced. Take it to any tailor. What will he charge you? Five dollars? Seven dollars? It's worth it.

"But, next time, you go to Maxi's. It'll wear like iron, believe you me. Tell them you work for me, and they'll reinforce the crotch on the house. They wouldn't charge you a penny."

Leighton's had just lost Vinnie as a cash customer. Jewish Sam put Vinnie on, right on the spot. There was no discussion of what Vinnie was to do or how he was to be paid.

Jewish Sam didn't talk to Vinnie. He talked to Joe Farts.

"Listen, if this guinea kid works out good, I owe you. Right now I need anybody who can work the street for me. Send me all the kids with headaches from The Avenue. I'll straighten them out. With me nobody has headaches."

Jewish Sam looked over at Tommy Fantone and grinned. Everybody knew what the look meant. Fantone was a merciless enforcer. Vinnie knew that with Jewish Sam and Fantone there would be no second chances. Jewish Sam let his people do just about anything except hold out on him.

It was a family-style dinner. The waiter brought out large platters of steak, pot roast and prime ribs, and they were passed around the long butcher-block table.

The food was good, but Vinnie was bored by the table conversation. Jewish Sam was as dull as Nunzi and the Moustache Petes on The Avenue. Maybe duller. Sam was talking endlessly about moving money, making investments, and borrowing and loaning out large sums. He was quoting interest rates and talking about mortgages. Vinnie could understand part of it. But most of the talk was confusing. Sam and Fantone and the people from East Flatbush were throwing around words and phrases that Vinnie had never heard before.

Vinnie looked over at Joe Farts, and Farts had a "beats-me" expression on his face. Farts was also so bloated by dessert time that he looked like he was barely holding on. He had taken off his tie and was holding a wet handkerchief to his forehead. His discomfort was beginning to annoy Fantone.

"You are a prick," Fantone said to Farts. "You got this fucking problem with your belly for as long as I know you. You'd think you would have the fucking brains to get yourself a G.I. series or an operation or something. I'm telling you, you're overdue. I'm sick of your problem, already. This is the last time I sit and try to eat a meal with you around."

Farts assured the quick-tempered Fantone that in a few minutes he would be all right. "I shouldn't have had so much, that's all, that's all. Don't worry."

Jewish Sam broke off his conversation with the East Flatbush people and turned to Vinnie.

"I'm thinking of putting you in as an area man out in East New York, kid. How are you with shvartzers?"

"Whatcha mean 'how I am with shvartzers?' If you're asking me if I get on with black dudes, it depends on the dudes. Some of Rufus Boyd's people, no problem. Some dudes I know out here are only ounce men, but they know the business and they're good dudes."

"Listen, kid, I'm not talking about shvartzers in junk. With your problem uptown, I'm not putting you near junk. You think I need trouble with your people? I'm talking about plain shvartzers, regular, ordinary, plain shvartzers. Can you work with them?"

"In what?"

"I want you showing shvartzers around in certain places in East New York where we got things going on, and I want shvartzer kids out playing in the street. Tommy will give you the blocks. We got a storefront out there and a phone. And my girl Ginger will be there starting next Monday. She'll know what I want done. Check with her every day."

"Wait a minute, Sam. I don't think I'm hearing you right. You want me bringing black dudes into East New York where they don't belong? That's suicide. Ain't you reading the papers? They got a war going out there. The Italians don't want niggers in East New York, and your people don't want them in Crown Heights. I bring niggers into East New York and Gallo's guys are going to put three in my head."

"Where you're going in East New York, Gallo don't care about. If any of the locals give you a problem, Tommy here will take care of it."

"You must got your reasons, Sam. But, it sounds like trouble. Big trouble."

"Listen, kid, you got a bad headache on The Avenue. If you want to work, the only work I got for you is with shvartzers. Would I put my girl Ginger in a storefront on Lavonia Avenue if we couldn't handle the situation? Don't be a shmuck."

Jewish Sam turned to Joe Farts. "Hey, Joey, what's the matter? I thought you said this kid here has got balls."

Farts answered quickly, "Don't worry, Sam, he'll work out, I'm telling you he'll work out."

That night and in the following weeks, Vinnie was introduced to a brand-new hustle. Farts was right. Jewish Sam was into action Vinnie knew nothing about. Jewish Sam was moving the profits of narcotics operations, loan sharking, and union racketeering into real-estate deals, deals Sam said were "so high class they're almost legit."

In the 1950s and early 1960s, Jewish Sam had made his reputation putting together legendary "bust outs," multimillion-dollar bankruptcy frauds that succeeded in draining off the assets of a half-dozen large Brooklyn businesses. Now, in the summer of 1969, Sam and other Brooklyn mobsters had figured out ways to bankrupt entire neighborhoods and make off with tens of millions of dollars.

The hustle involved gaining control of thousands of one- and two-family homes in the East New York, Crown Heights, and East Flatbush sections of Brooklyn. In 1969, these areas were still predominantly white. But homeowners in these areas had reason to fear that blacks from nearby Bedford-Stuyvesant and Brownsville would soon be moving into their neighborhoods. Sam and the other real-estate hustlers knew this and did their best to heighten racial tensions and fears. Their objective was to cause panic in white neighborhoods so homeowners would sell out in a hurry to real-estate agents and fronts controlled by Sam and other mobsters.

Narcotics money and other mob funds in need of laundering were put into all-cash deals to buy thousands of one- and two-family homes in East New York and other "changing" areas of Brooklyn. Vinnie and other punks were hired to "showboat shvartzers" in these areas—to get black people walking around white areas or driving through on whatever pretense.

All this was part of what came to be known as blockbusting. An important part of blockbusting was creating a climate of panic. Sam and the others were trying to get a message across to white homeowners: "Sell out now while your house is still worth top dollar. When the niggers start moving in, you won't be able to give it away."

Now, one might ask, why were Sam and half the narcotics dealers and loan sharks in the city in a hurry to buy up one- and two-family homes in lower-middle-class neighborhoods in Brooklyn? From a hustler's point of view in that summer of 1969 those houses represented gold, pure gold.

The whole hustling scheme was hatched after mob accountants figured out ways to rip off a well-intentioned provision of Lyndon Johnson's War on Poverty program. The Johnson administration had created a program that was supposed to make it easier for blacks and other minority group members to obtain home-mortgage loans. On paper it looked good. Any member of a minority group who had a good employment and credit record could go to a bank or finance company and get a home-mortgage loan that would be guaranteed, in effect co-signed, by the government through the Federal Housing Administration.

If the recipient of the loan defaulted, the FHA would make good on the loan in full to the bank or finance company. This was thought of as progressive social legislation.

The only trouble was that when the government put its new FHA program into operation, mob hustlers quickly figured out ways to rip it off and defeat its purposes.

As a precinct cop and a detective in the 1960s, I saw the same thing happen again and again: the government in Washington would create an antipoverty program, and the hustlers in the neighborhoods would rip it off. The FHA program of guaranteed mortgage loans, the Neighborhood Youth Corps program, and various other well-intentioned antipoverty projects were bankrupted and discredited by neighborhood mobsters. Poor people who were supposed to be the beneficiaries of the programs were set up—victimized by the very programs that were designed to help them.

The FHA racket was among the most loathsome. It looted the federal treasury of billions of dollars, destroyed entire neighborhoods, wiped out the meager savings of tens of thousands of little people, dangerously intensified racial fears, and kept punks like Jewish Sam and Vinnie in clover for years.

There were many variations on the FHA hustle, but this was essentially the way it worked: Jewish Sam and the other real-estate "speculators," as they called themselves, ran big ads in the *Amsterdam News* and other black and Spanish-language newspapers and offered large apartments at low rentals. The ads were phonies. There were no such apartments. The ads were come-ons, to get blacks to the store-front real-estate offices of the speculators. The whole idea was to draw apartment-seeking blacks into white areas and to sell them houses they really couldn't afford. Blacks were told about "the great new deal from the government." The blockbusters said, in effect, "We'll put you into a house. Just leave it to us."

By creating black traffic in white neighborhoods, it was that much easier for the blockbusters to buy out white home-owners at panic prices. Once the whites were out of their houses, bribes were paid to FHA officials and appraisers to get quick mortgage loans for the black clients of the block-busters. The bribes also bought appraisals for much more than the houses were really worth.

All of this would happen at great speed. The blockbuster could, for example, lay out eighteen thousand dollars on the first of April to buy a house from a white family and then sell the house to a black family for thirty thousand two or three weeks later.

All too often, the black family would move into the house only to find some months later that they could not keep up the mortgage payments.* The bank would foreclose on the mortgage. The black family would be evicted possibly after losing whatever savings they had. The government would pay off the bank and take title to the house. And the rest was a hustler's dream. The government would sell the house at auction and the blockbusters would buy the house again and resell it again, with FHA backing, to another and yet another black family. Working this way, the blockbusters were able to "churn," sell and resell, the same house as many as ten times in two or three years and to realize tens of thousands of dollars for their trouble. The regional director of the Federal Housing Administration, Donald Carroll, was in on the hustle and later went to jail. The banks looked the other way or took part in the action themselves. The FBI did nothing until there was a Senate investigation. And Vinnie and many like him found criminal jobs in blockbusting and related rackets that were even better paying than the jobs they had in the heroin business.

Vinnie moved out of the apartment on Pleasant Avenue again and became a protégé of Jewish Sam in the real-estate rackets. And for him there were to be many nights of steak and roast beef at Luger's. In the storefront on Lavonia Avenue, Ginger would send out for Chinese food to celebrate a particularly profitable closing on a house. Vinnie got on well

---

*The blockbuster almost always prepared the FHA mortgage application for the prospective black homeowner. If the applicant's employment record was not good, the blockbuster made up a phony employment record and, if necessary, submitted phony credit information. As a result, the government approved loans to thousands of blacks who could not possibly keep up the mortgage payments.

with Ginger and began to show her a life that Stella had only dreamed about.

No longer was Vinnie stuck up in the apartment on 112th Street or out wading at Orchard Beach. He was, as he boasted to Joe Farts, "nigger rich."

11. Telling It to the *Times*

Life, as the old man knew it, had not changed. Vinnie was again working with hoodlums and Ernie Boy was still on The Avenue moving heroin packages. The wiseguys were still on top. His conversations with me, the risks he had taken, had meant nothing. I thought the old man would lose all hope, but he didn't. He kept in touch by telephone, and we talked for hours about Vinnie and the latest doings on The Avenue.

Through the summer and fall of 1969, I made no progress on the case. I had information, but I had no real way of turning that information into evidence—not without the help of SIU. When I called SIU, detectives would tell me that Tange or another boss from the Narcotics Division would get back to me. They never did.

Jay Kriegel was off working in John Lindsay's reelection campaign.

At City Hall, the campaign crowded out other matters. When Lindsay and Leary did sit down together at the mayor's weekly cabinet meetings, they talked mostly about progress on the construction of a new police headquarters building, about the acquisition of new scooters and radio cars, and about the installation of new emergency communications systems. People who attended these meetings said there were no discussions about corruption or integrity problems in the Narcotics Division or elsewhere in the department.

Clearly, no one in high authority in the police department or in city government was paying much attention to my pleas for an investigation of Pleasant Avenue. And, there was also official indifference on another matter I had brought to Kriegel's attention.

A fellow police officer, Frank Serpico, had firsthand knowledge of ongoing police collusion and pay-offs in organized crime gambling operations in the Bronx and in Brooklyn. Frank shared his information with me and together we tried to get the department and the mayor to investigate corruption in plainclothes units in which Frank was working. As readers of the book about Frank's life know, this effort was as unavailing as my efforts to get the department to go against Pleasant Avenue and SIU.

A few days before the mayoral election, the New York *Daily News* published the results of its much-respected straw poll. It showed Lindsay in the lead.

I rushed to Kriegel's office in the basement of City Hall. I remember saying to Jay: "Lindsay's going to win. You don't have to worry about the election anymore. Now you can do something about corruption. You can get rid of Leary, who isn't doing anything about it, and do what has to be done."

Kriegel appeared startled. His only response was, "I never promised we'd get rid of Howard, David."

We both knew what that meant. It was all bullshit. The ride to Pleasant Avenue. Everything. It was all a stall. Even with a reelection victory, Lindsay was not going to pursue "the corruption issue."

I turned quickly and walked out. I never spoke to Kriegel again.

It was late afternoon, and I had an appointment to give a talk to a group of graduate students in the office of Lindsay's deputy mayor, Robert Sweet. The students were serving in the mayor's Urban Fellows program. They were getting on-the-job training in the ways of municipal government working as aides to various city officials.

For six hours, I poured out my guts to these young people. There was one young fellow there from Columbia University. He was tall and wore granny glasses. He sat near me on my left. As I talked about my frustrations in trying to do my job, he began to bow his head, and, as I went on further about the department and about other men who saw themselves trapped in a system of deceit and sham, this fellow in the granny glasses began to cry. The sincerity of this gangling kid from Columbia touched me, really touched me. I don't know his name, but I owe him, and I owe the other young people in that room. All of us there that evening drew strength from one another.

Later that night, I decided that I had gone as far as I could within the chain of command in trying to get my superiors in the department to do something about Pleasant Avenue and about SIU and about everything that Serpico had experienced in plainclothes work. Kriegel had made it clear that the mayor was not about to intervene in what City Hall considered to be the department's own business. The cover-up, I was convinced, would continue unless Lindsay or Leary were forced to do something about it.

I decided that at least part of the story had to be told publicly. I had talked in confidence about corruption in the department with David Burnham, a reporter for the *New York Times.* That night, I called Burnham and told him I was ready to talk for publication. And I told him I was sure other members of the department would come forward and tell what they knew in the hope that the job could be made clean.

Burnham and his editors at the *Times* met with Serpico and myself and a small group of other officers. The *Times* conducted its own extensive investigation and, as mentioned in an earlier chapter, on April 25, 1970, it began to publish a series of page-one stories on corruption in the police department. The truth was no longer bottled up in Jay Kriegel's basement office at City Hall. David Burnham's stories did not go deeply into narcotics corruption, but they did contain a good deal of information on what was going on in the precincts and in the plainclothes squads assigned to control bookmaking and policy operations.

Publication of the corruption stories, the appointment of the Knapp Commission, and talk around the city of a forthcoming crackdown on corruption did nothing to slow activity on Pleasant Avenue, or within SIU. Heroin dealers in East Harlem and in the police department saw no reason to change their ways. Despite the appointment of the Knapp Commission, the wiseguys scoring heroin money still felt safe.

The Knapp investigators concentrated their efforts on small-potatoes precinct corruption and on cops who were tied to gamblers and pimps and prostitutes. It made much of liquor-law violations and after-hours bars and unlicensed sidewalk vendors, and it took cops to task for taking free meals or free lodging at hotels. In short, it went after low-level "high visibility" forms of corruption. The cop on the beat was the major target. Why? What about the captains and inspectors? What about SIU? What about the DAs and the judges who sold cases? What about a mayor who wouldn't meet with cops ready to talk about corruption?

And, from the beginning, the commission's chief counsel, Michael F. Armstrong, made it plain to me that he did not plan to call me as a witness. "If we put you on, Durk," Armstrong said, "I'm going to have to call Leary and Walsh and Lindsay. It'll take three days of hearing time, and I just don't have that much time to give to it with everything else."

The Commission set out to nail the cop on the beat. A prominent trial lawyer told me, "They'll never put you on. Serpico isn't a threat. But, you want to talk about bosses and lawyers and judges and the mayor. That's another ball-game." But because of pressure from the press and the public and a member of the City Council, I was called to testify before the Knapp Commission.

12. Undercover in SIU

October 5, 1970, was a big day in my life. It was a big day in Bob Leuci's life. And it was the day in which the cover-up of heroin dealing on Pleasant Avenue and in SIU really began to come apart.

Early that day, Leuci and I met in a hallway outside the district attorney's office in Brooklyn. I was excited. I had just been applauded and cheered by members of a Brooklyn grand jury after giving testimony on corruption charges involving my former commanding officer in the Department of Investigation, Captain Phillip Foran.

I had told the grand jury about taking Frank Serpico to see Foran and about Foran's reaction when Frank told him about corruption in a Brooklyn plainclothes unit. Foran had said that Frank could either forget about what he had seen or he could make formal charges and take the risk of finding himself "floating face down in the East River." Foran was a captain commanding an anticorruption unit, and this was his reaction to a patrolman reporting corruption.*

The grand jury's reaction to my testimony on Foran had sent me out of the jury room in a high state of exhilaration.

*Foran was not indicted. In a departmental trial, he was found guilty of perjury charges growing out of the Serpico affair. Later he became president of the Captains' Endowment Association, which represents all officers of the rank of captain and above in the department.

The truth was finally starting to come out. At last, the public would begin to get some information on how cops really lived day to day. Secrecy, bottling up corruption allegations in Kriegel's office, or Walsh's office, or Leary's office, made possible the illusion that everything was all right in the department when it wasn't. The public had to know that there was more to police work than building a new headquarters, or buying new radio cars or walkie-talkies, or patrolling the Belt Parkway, or running the PAL. The department had to be open and responsive. And it had to stand for decency and integrity, or it stood for nothing.

The adrenalin was really flowing when I spotted Bob Leuci walking toward me in the hallway.

As soon as we made eye contact, Leuci could see that I was way up. I grabbed hold of his arm and said to him: "Look, you're going to talk." There was no time for pussyfooting around. There was no time for bullshitting. Leuci knew it and I knew it.

Leuci didn't hesitate. He said to me quietly, "Okay, David."

We walked down the hall to the office of Irving Seidman, chief of the rackets division in the Brooklyn DA's office.

Seidman expected me. I was supposed to have lunch with him.

Leuci told Seidman that I had come to SIU with information on large-scale heroin dealing on Pleasant Avenue.

I asked Leuci to tell Seidman exactly what SIU had done with my information. Leuci hesitated a moment and then told Seidman, "The information was probably very good, but nothing was done with it."

Seidman asked Leuci if he had any knowledge of money ever being passed to cops in SIU to head off narcotics investigations.

Leuci said, "No."

There was then a discussion of Tange's warning to Leuci

about not cooperating with me. Leuci remembered Tange saying, "Durk's fucking case is not going to go anywhere. Is that understood? We're not going to put wires in on Pleasant Avenue and get KG's and cops talking about a pad. That's what Durk is really trying to get us to do."

Seidman said that Leuci should talk to a prosecutor in Manhattan.

I asked Leuci to go with me to see Seidman's counterpart in Manhattan, Kenneth Conboy.

Leuci said, "We keep doing this, Dave, and I'm going to land up in a fucking grand jury." Leuci knew he was getting into heavy stuff. But, he got into my car, and we drove over to Manhattan.

Leuci talked to Conboy and to Larry Goldman, another assistant district attorney. Conboy asked me to leave the room while he questioned Leuci. Goldman later said Conboy wanted specifics, and Leuci didn't give him specifics.

There was the usual lawyer-to-cop lecture on the difference between information and evidence.

I pleaded with Conboy. "Listen, you got a narcotics detective here willing to talk to you about a major operation being burned. I'm not asking for indictments. I'm asking for an investigation."

I could not get Conboy to order a full-scale investigation. He wanted specifics from Leuci before he would put the DA's detective squad on the case.

We left Conboy's office hungry, tired, and down. Leuci was jittery. "Dave, that guy looks right through you. He's sharp. What are you getting me into?"

Leuci wanted to back me up, to help me get an investigation started on the wiseguys on Pleasant Avenue, but he didn't want to be thrown into a grand jury to testify against SIU. While Leuci was in with Conboy, I saw that there was an interview in the paper with Manhattan District Attorney

Frank Hogan. In the interview, Hogan described First Deputy Police Commissioner John Walsh as "a saint of a man" and said Walsh would never tolerate corruption. Hogan also said Walsh would be an excellent successor to Leary. The Hogan statement came soon after Leary's rather abrupt announcement that he had decided to resign as police commissioner. I thought that Walsh was not following up on allegations of corruption as vigorously as he should. Hogan's statement seemed naïve to me. If Leuci saw the Hogan interview, would he believe that anyone in the police department or the D.A.'s office was truly interested in hearing about corruption at SIU? I hid the newspaper from Leuci.

Leuci was losing his patience with me.

"David, you just don't know shit about what it is to be in narcotics. You don't even know what it is to be a cop. How many years you on the job? And, I'm telling you, you're still not a cop. You've been down in the D of I working Mickey Mouse cases. That's not being a cop."

Leuci was putting me down the same way the old man had. I didn't know all the Funzis. I was some sort of freak from an Ivy League college who'd gotten it in his head to be a cop. I didn't know what I was up against. I didn't know the street. I didn't know the department. And I didn't know what the system did with troublemakers. In short, I was Don Quixote with a badge and a gun. And Leuci didn't want to play the role of Sancho Panza to a nudgy Quixote who could take him right over a cliff.

But, that very afternoon, when I asked Bob Leuci to come with me to the Knapp Commission, he went. Tired and haggard and scared, he went. Leuci was hooked.

With all his bitching, and with all his put-downs of me, Leuci was not about to bail out. His visit to the Knapp offices that day was followed by several more visits. And, after stormy confrontations with a Knapp Commission lawyer and federal officials, he began to tell in detail what he knew about SIU and agreed to work undercover to make cases against those in the police department and elsewhere who were involved in narcotics corruption. These investigations led to the downfall of the SIU.

Why Leuci did what he did, when he did it, I don't know. He went with me to Seidman and Conboy and the Knapp Commission soon after he learned someone very close to him had a heroin habit. This discovery must have had a profound effect on him. There he was in SIU where cops were selling heroin cases, and now he knew someone personally who was a junkie. Maybe that was enough reason for what he did with me. It's hard for me to know. Bob Leuci is a very complicated guy, as complicated as everybody else, that is.

I don't think Bob ever made a calculated decision to turn against SIU and cooperate with me and the Knapp Commission and to work with the Feds. I don't know if he would ever have come forward if he wasn't asked to. What he did wasn't done without tears and without pain. Certainly a meeting that took place one Sunday afternoon in my apartment with me and Henry Ruth brought him further along the path.

In agreeing to work as an undercover agent against the hustlers in SIU, Bob Leuci put everything on the line. Anyone looking at what he did before October 5, 1970, must also look at what he did on that day and every day since. Leuci was able at last to see himself and how the heady atmosphere of SIU had changed him. "How did I ever get to be in this situation?" he asked himself at one point. "How did it all happen? I used to feel lousy in high school if I cut a class to go out for a smoke. That's the kind of kid I was. Then I'm in SIU and cops are taking money and selling heroin, and I'm doing things with them . . . We had the wrong heroes in SIU but, at the time, they were the only heroes around."

Bob Leuci knew the high price of corruption for the corrupted. Two men he scored heroin money with in SIU took their lives with their own service revolvers when they knew they were about to face criminal prosecution. Others went off to a federal penitentiary.

Bob Leuci knew what Jay Kriegel and John Lindsay didn't want to know. Leuci knew the truth about SIU. He knew the schizophrenia of men who made good arrests one night and who sold heroin the next. He knew that scoring heroin money could become as addictive as heroin itself. And, he knew that the heroin his relative was buying in the streets of Queens might be SIU heroin.

Bob Leuci's decision to go with me to the Knapp Commission on October 5, 1970, marked the beginning of the end for SIU. But, despite all that Bob said at the time to the Knapp lawyers, to Ken Conboy in Hogan's office, and to federal investigators, another year would go by before anything was done about Pleasant Avenue.

13. The Convent Avenue Case

"They're cutting the stuff in a new place on 119th right off The Avenue towards the river. You could lay across the street and catch 'em nice."

"I told you about the cop who picks up for the captain? He's a bad one. He's dealing pieces now, thirty-eights, right on The Avenue."

"Where's the pictures for me, David? You got the pictures yet of the guys who go with those plate numbers?"

> —Excerpts from telephone
> conversations with the
> old man

"I've been in bed with some of these SIU guys for seven years now. You know how many doors we knocked down together? And now I'm going to get them all locked up. It all sucks."

"There's not stomachs or livers or anuses that can take this kind of pressure."

"The Feds are killing me. They got me with a finger up a tiger's ass on the dead run and holding on by one ear."

"Does the commissioner know? Does he know why I'm doing it? I want him to know."*

—Excerpts from telephone
conversations with Bob Leuci

January, 1971.
It was now nearly two years since the old man had come to me for help. The Cadillacs and Lincolns were still double- and triple-parked outside the storefronts on Pleasant Avenue. Zanfardino and Gigi and the other Moustache Petes were going about their business just as they had for years.

The old man didn't know much about what Vinnie was doing. "All I know is that he's got an apartment in Queens, David. He's in a fancy apartment house with a doorman and everything. And, he's living with a Ginger. I never even met her, but she's nice to me on the telephone. I call and I don't even speak to him. I speak to her. I don't know what kind of girl she is. She could be a nigger for all I know. But, at least, thank God, Vinnie isn't on The Avenue. And after what he did with Nunzi and that cunt Stella, I don't think he's doing packages.

"One night, out of the blue, Vinnie called me late and said there was some trouble. This was just two weeks ago. He was in a fight in a park in Queens, and a kid got shot. Another kid I used to know from the neighborhood got taken in for it. Vinnie was all upset. Two days later he calls me and tells me money was passed and everything's all right with this other kid, a punk with a father who is also a punk. I don't even know why he called me the first time. Maybe if they couldn't

---

*Leuci wanted Police Commissioner Patrick Murphy to know that he (Leuci) was not out to embarrass the department. Murphy had taken over from Leary when Leary abruptly quit in the early days of the Knapp Commission investigation.

fix it up, maybe he wanted me to speak to someone on The Avenue. When they got trouble, they remember a father. If they don't have trouble, I talk to Ginger. Where is he? He's out. When's he coming back? She don't know."

Once, at a critical moment, Bob Leuci asked me to meet him at an isolated spot near an airport. He needed someone to talk to. Leuci was terrified. He was working against people who would pick up quickly on any mistake he made. He'd stay up most of the night reliving the day before and planning the next day. How could he work against so many wiseguys, he wondered night after night, and get away with it. And, after it was all over, what then? Where would he live? Could he still work the job? Did the police commissioner understand what he was doing? Would other cops understand and believe that he was not a rat?

Leuci was shaky. One night he said he had almost been killed that day working with the Feds on some mob guys in the Little Italy section of lower Manhattan.

"These guys got on to me, David. How? I don't know. And, later we got them on a wire talking with this wiseguy who I know who owes me. These guys tell him they are going to do a job on me and he doesn't say much. All he tells them is that if they do something to me they better be right. That's all he says. That's what saves me—his saying they better be right. He's a big guy down there, and they didn't want to do anything to me and be wrong. So they must of not been that sure I was a wrong-o, and they went ahead and did business with me. But that's how close I'm coming, David. That's how close I'm coming."

Bob Leuci in SIU and the old man on Pleasant Avenue kept me in touch. Their day-to-day reports from two of the country's busiest heroin markets had a profound effect on my own police work. When I received information on drug dealing, I knew enough not to refer anything anymore to SIU.

Sending a case to SIU made about as much sense as referring it to Abbamonte or Zanfardino.

I was careful about what I did with all narcotics-related information.

One night, I was at a party at the Tavern-on-the-Green Restaurant in Central Park. A guest, a matronly woman, became excited when she found out that I was a detective. She took me aside to say in a low voice that her maid lived in Harlem and somehow had learned the identities of a number of gentlemen who were dealing kilos of heroin from a location near the Convent Avenue campus of City College. The woman said her maid had called the Narcotics Division several times with the information. "But it doesn't seem to do any good. The dope pushers are still there, Sergeant Durk."

The woman was indignant and wanted me to tell her right there why the department had not done anything with her maid's information. I asked her if she would care to give me the information and took out my pad and ballpoint pen.

The next day, needless to say, I didn't call SIU, the Narcotics Division, or the police commissioner. Instead, I called Larry Goldman in Frank Hogan's office. I remember saying, "Larry, take out your pad and make a scratch. I've got information for you on a possible kilo-heroin operation on Convent Avenue. You can be damn sure I'm not giving it to SIU, so you're going to take it."

Goldman took it. He asked two detectives who happened to be in the DA's office at the time to take a ride up to Convent Avenue to see what they could find. The two detectives were at the location for only a short time when they spotted two of the suspects. The detectives were able to seize Alvin Kirks and Ali Akbar and one kilo of heroin.

With Goldman I got direct action. I didn't have to go from one commissioner with flags in his office to another commissioner with flags in his office. And, I didn't have to suffer the ire of a Narcotics Division captain who was angry with me for bringing him unsolicited information.

And there was more to the Convent Avenue case. The arrests of Kirks and Akbar later led to the arrest of a third defendant, a rather famous lady, Doll Rae Mapp. Ms. Mapp had figured in a earlier case that had led to a landmark decision by the United States Supreme Court.*

As icing on the cake, Akbar and Kirks had allegedly tried to bribe Goldman's detectives. The detectives went along with the alleged bribery scheme long enough to discover where Akbar and Kirks had hidden a cache of stolen merchandise. As a final irony, the stolen merchandise was hidden in an apartment in the building in which Larry Goldman lived.

"It's fantastic, David," Goldman said. "This guy Kirks was my neighbor. He lived two floors from me, and his apartment was loaded with swag from twenty burglaries."

In the Convent Avenue case we were lucky. It was most unusual to seize so much heroin without weeks of under-cover work, round-the-clock surveillance and wiretapping. The case was as easy as it was because Kirks and Akbar were not careful about how and when they made large heroin deliveries.

When Goldman's detectives went up to Convent Avenue, they had only one key bit of information. They were told to look for a Buick Riviera with Ohio plates. When they spotted

---

*Mapp v. Ohio, 367 U.S. 643. The U.S. Supreme Court reversed the judgment of the Ohio Supreme Court, which had reaffirmed conviction of Ms. Mapp for possession of obscene materials. Taking note of the fact that the police did not have a proper warrant for entering Ms. Mapp's apartment, during which raid the obscene materials were discovered, the U.S. Supreme Court ruled that as a matter of due process evidence obtained by a search and seizure in violation of the Fourth Amendment was inadmissible in state courts as well as in federal courts.

the car, they walked toward it. Kirks was in the car and saw them coming. He panicked and threw a plastic bag containing the kilo of heroin into the street. All the detectives had to do was pick up the bag and cuff Kirks and his companion, Akbar.

We couldn't expect to be so lucky on Pleasant Avenue. The Moustache Petes who ran heroin businesses on The Avenue were cautious men. They employed a small army of lookouts, mainly children and women. The Avenue was only six blocks long. If the lookouts saw anyone who even looked remotely like "the man," word was passed, and heroin packages were kept off the street. Even the old man didn't know which car would actually be carrying the stuff and which car was a decoy. In the cutting rooms, heroin was stockpiled in secret wall compartments and behind Charlie Chan-type revolving shelves. And multi-kilo packages were shipped out on holidays or early on weekend mornings when few people were around. The Capras and Zanfardinos knew their business. They had been doing it for years. They would never be as careless as Kirks and Akbar. It would take more than Goldman's detectives to bring down The Avenue.

The news media were interested in my efforts to persuade students on college campuses to become policemen. *Life* magazine had done a picture layout on my college trips and, in the spring of 1971, the *New York Times* sent a reporter along with me on a recruiting trip to California.

On the Berkeley campus, I was the target of an antiestablishment, antipig demonstration. I was supposed to give a speech at the university's Center for Law and Social Policy. At the last minute, the speech was canceled. A university spokesman was apologetic: "We're sorry to cancel you out, sergeant, but we have a problem. If we allow you to talk, the students have threatened to burn down the building."

In the New York City Police Department I was looked upon by many as a radical and as a troublemaker. On the turbulent Berkeley campus, I was seen as an establishment pig. Marty Arnold, the reporter for the *Times* who was with me, thought it was all funny. At the time, I didn't think so.

After my misadventure in Berkeley, I went back to New York and was asked to talk about police recruitment on an interview program given Sunday mornings on NBC. At one point, the interviewer, Joseph Michaels, questioned me about the Knapp Commission's investigation of police corruption. Michaels wanted to know specifically if I thought there was any truth to reports that cops were involved in narcotics corruption. I told him I thought the reports were true and went on to tell him part of the story of SIU and Pleasant Avenue. And, in a guarded way, about the old man and about Vinnie.

This was the first time I'd talked in public, in any way, about the old man and Pleasant Avenue. The next day, the *New York Times* carried an account of my remarks, and two weeks later the Chief of Detectives Albert Seedman went on the same program to respond to what I had said about SIU's failure to follow up on information I'd provided about East Harlem heroin dealing. Seedman said that there was "nothing to Durk's charges," that all I'd said about SIU was "vague and nebulous."

Immediately after Seedman's television appearance, I called Deputy Police Commissioner Robert Daley. I told Daley, "Either the chief is dangerously misinformed, or he's a liar." Daley said he would speak to Seedman.

Several days later, Police Commissioner Murphy ordered two separate high-level investigations of my charges against SIU. One of the investigations was to be carried out personally by Assistant Chief Inspector Arthur Grubert, the department's new chief of intelligence.

I knew Grubert and trusted him. When Grubert asked to

see me, I told him everything, beginning with day one, beginning with that snowy Sunday afternoon in February, 1969,
when I went to see the old man in East Harlem. I told Grubert
about Vinnie, Ernie Boy, Capra, Gigi, and all the Moustache
Petes on The Avenue. I showed him diagrams of the back
areas of storefronts and abandoned buildings where the old
man said heroin was cut and stored. I showed him my list of
license plate numbers. I told him about my visits to SIU and
about Tange's threats.

Grubert was patient and methodical. I decided to go all the
way with him.

"Chief, I've never let anybody meet my informant, but if
you'll go, I'll take you to see him."

Early in July, 1971, Chief Grubert, Inspector Paul Delise,
and I drove out to a restaurant parking lot in the Bayside
section of Queens to meet the old man.

When we arrived, the old man was leaning against the
fender of a car in the restaurant lot, reading a newspaper. I
called to him, and he got into the back seat of my car next
to Chief Grubert.

"Hello, Dave. We don't have to worry, nobody knows me
out here. The pressmen's union once had their dinner in this
place. If you're in the neighborhood again, the veal scalop-
pine ain't bad."

After meeting with the old man secretly for more than two
years, I felt uneasy sitting with him with Grubert and Delise
there. And I was sure that the old man was also uncomfort-
able. But he didn't let on.

I made the introductions. I told the old man that I trusted
Grubert and Delise completely and that they were there because they wanted to help.

"You can talk to them just like you talk to me," I said.

"All right, Dave," he said, "I understand. What do you want
to know?"

"Just tell them about your son and about Ernie Boy and

everything that's going on on The Avenue."

I wanted the old man to make it clear to Grubert that the KG's in East Harlem, the men known to the department as bookmakers, numbers men, and loan sharks were also major figures in heroin. I asked the old man if this was true.

"Sure, David, it's true. You still don't know it's true? How many times I got to tell you? I told you that the first time you came up to The Avenue.

"When I was coming up on The Avenue, it was all different," the old man said. "Somebody in drugs was a guy you stayed away from. I remember I was working for a numbers man and he seen me talking to a guy who hung around with dope dealers. The numbers guy liked me, and you know what he did? He come over to me right on the street corner and slapped my face. In front of the whole Avenue, he slapped my face. Then I knew I was wrong to talk to that drug guy. But now the numbers guys and the drug guys, they are all the same people.

"Listen, Mr. Grubert, I'm not going to tell you I've been an angel. Now, I'm not a guy who goes out bouncing. But, when I was a kid, you think I didn't want action? You think there wasn't action on The Avenue then? I wasn't even thirty yet and maybe I had like twenty-five thousand dollars in my own money out on the street in shylocking. And, the interest came to a couple a thousand a week. And, I did the collecting myself. You don't have an angel here. But, I seen what the needle does. I've had one kid die already in my arms. So that's why I've been trying with David to get a fucking punk like Ernie Boy put away. That's all I want. You should take Ernie Boy and put his ass in Sing Sing.

"You told Mr. Grubert about my sitdown with Nunzi, David? And, how I went to Joe Pelham Bays and got Nunzi to stop talking about the coffins. You tell Mr. Grubert all that?"

I nodded and told the old man it was important to give

Grubert and Delise whatever specific information he had.

The old man began talking about the Hole. "That's what they call it. The Hole. That's where I think the heavy cutting is going on. That's what I hear from The Avenue. There's a secret panel in the back of a candy store on Pleasant, on the west side of The Avenue. The panel is built on wheels and it swings away. You got to press buttons and then in the back behind the panel they got chairs and a table there for cutting.

"And, there's another place that's very important. It's not on Pleasant. It's over on First Avenue. Two brothers run it. It's a bakery. You know the place I mean?"

Delise said, "It's got to be the place on the west side of First. I've been sitting on that joint myself as a possible numbers bank. The place looks like money. And there's too much traffic in and out of there for a bakery. I don't care how good the stuff is."

"That's right, that's right," the old man said. "They're moving big packages in and out of there all day. One of the brothers is married to a real good looker. I think she used to be Miss Puerto Rico or Miss Mexico. I mean this is some woman. She drives around with a trunk full of the stuff. They deal with the Cubans down on Fourteenth Street, and she takes the packages to them."

Delise turned to Grubert. "Chief, I know that location very well. We've been across the street on a rooftop watching it. And it's got activity that's just not called for in that neighborhood for a legit business. Half the customers are coming out of Cadillacs and Thunderbirds. There's money and a hustle in that place. There's got to be."

The old man looked at his watch. "I've got to leave soon, David. I'll be late for work. It's a good half hour on the subway from here back to the city."

I asked the old man to tell Grubert and Delise quickly about the cop in East Harlem who was selling guns on The Avenue.

And I asked him to bring me up-to-date on Vinnie. The old man gave Grubert the name of the cop who he said was dealing guns, and he said he had witnessed one gun sale himself.

"And, about Vinnie, what can I tell you? So he ain't doing anything anymore with Ernie Boy, but there are other Ernie Boys, and I didn't tell you, David, but I think he didn't learn a lesson yet. He's running with some very bad people. That kid who shot the other kid in the park? I think that's Vinnie's new Ernie Boy."

The old man said he really had to get to work. I thanked him for meeting with Grubert. And I told him I would be in touch.

14. The Gun-Selling Cop

The timing of the old man's meeting with Chief Grubert could not have been better. It was superb. Grubert, with the full backing of Commissioner Murphy, had just put together his own narcotics intelligence unit. And detectives in Grubert's unit, following leads from the Bronx and Westchester, had already identified Capra and Inglese as major figures in the heroin business.

Grubert had a lieutenant, three sergeants, and fifteen detectives watching Capra, Inglese, and a number of the very people the old man was talking about. But Grubert's undercover squad wasn't working Pleasant Avenue. They didn't know about Pleasant Avenue. The squad was sitting on a social club on Westchester Avenue in the Bronx. The club was located in an old butcher shop and there was still a sign outside that read "Wilkenson Meat Market."

What Grubert didn't know at the time was that the Wilkenson really was only a social club. The men who ran the Pleasant Avenue heroin establishment went there to play cards and to unwind. Heavy Pleasant Avenue heroin shipments to the Bronx, Grubert later learned, didn't go to Wilkenson, they went to another Italian social club, the Beach Rose on White Plains Road.

Grubert moved cautiously. He didn't want to tip his hand, and he didn't want to offend the Narcotics Division or Chief of Detectives Seedman, who had said my information on East Harlem heroin dealing was vague and nebulous.

The old man's information was dynamite. Grubert knew just how valuable it could be. The old man had identified major New York multi-kilo dealers—Capra, Zanfardino, Inglese, and others. He'd given Grubert hard information on where the heavy cutting was going on, and he'd identified a "Mr. A" as the moneyman behind Capra and Zanfardino. Also, in discussing Vinnie's activities, he'd given Grubert an odds-and-ends assortment of tidbits on organized crime.

Grubert overlooked nothing. He set out to get all the Ernie Boys he could, on The Avenue and off The Avenue.

For me, the summer of 1971 was as exciting as hell. Grubert was very interested in Vinnie's activities. Vinnie was involved in a criminal operation that cannot be described here without endangering others. Grubert assigned a team of twenty-seven detectives to go after the punks that Vinnie was running with. The team worked around-the-clock, seven days a week all summer, and gathered enough evidence to put away thirty members of organized crime families. This whole case came from just one of the old man's tidbits.

Then there was the matter of the cop the old man said was selling guns to hoodlums on The Avenue.

Grubert and I really wanted this bastard badly.

I asked Grubert for authorization to have the old man buy a gun from the cop or from one of the cop's street dealers. Grubert didn't hesitate. He said, "Sure, go ahead."

I met with the old man and gave him a hundred dollars to buy a gun.

Several days later, the old man called me and said he had the gun and he asked me what I wanted him to do with it. I asked him if he could bring the gun to my apartment. He said he would.

When the old man called on a Sunday afternoon, the

household was in turmoil. My elder daughter was celebrating her birthday, her tenth, and a party was just beginning. Guests were already arriving, and the living room was becoming a sea of ecstatic, squealing ten-year-old girls. Since I thought the old man would take at least an hour to get over to the apartment, I left for a few minutes to pick up a station wagon I'd rented to transport my daughter and her friends. But the old man made it over much faster than I'd expected. He must have been very anxious to turn over the gun. Arlene was certainly somewhere in the middle of the high tide, so one of the guests must have opened the door for him. When I returned, he was standing nervously in the foyer and clutching tightly a small brown paper bag that held the gun. Headed for the pressroom in his work pants and a multicolored, sleeveless undershirt, he was not really dressed for a party. Before I got to him, another of my daughter's guests entered with her parents. The mother, who'd never met me, stood for a long, awkward moment before the old man. Finally, she said to him warmly, but with a question in her voice, "How do you do . . . Mr. Durk?" The old man shot back, smiling, "Pleased to meet you." It all happened so naturally and improbably that I'll cherish forever this crazy moment of humor in the midst of buzzing chaos.

The old man was amused and said later, "Maybe she thought I was the grandfather, David."

"No," I said, "she made you right away as the Sicilian Charlie Chaplin."

The old man gave me the small brown paper bag. The gun in it wasn't a cheap Saturday Night Special. It was a standard, five-shot snub-nosed revolver of the type generally carried by uniformed policemen while off duty and by detectives and plainclothesmen on duty.

At the time, many guns of this kind were being reported

stolen from policemen's lockers in many station houses. And I knew that the theft of guns from lockers was a particular problem in the 25th Precinct in East Harlem.

The old man said he hadn't been able to buy the gun directly from the cop he knew was dealing. The cop wouldn't deal with him directly. The old man gave the money to a girl who worked as a waitress on The Avenue and knew the cop well. The gun had been delivered to the old man by a neighborhood kid who was a runner for the wiseguys. I had the gun. I had the cop's name. The old man had seen the cop making an earlier sale of four guns, but there was nothing yet to tie the cop directly to the sale of *this* gun. The cop had been smart enough to insulate himself from the actual street sale. And the girl to whom the old man had given the money had not delivered the gun. This was the standard way of doing business on The Avenue. The actual supplier of drugs or guns rarely delivered the merchandise himself. The Ernie Boys and Vinnies would be used for deliveries. If an Ernie Boy was busted or ripped off in making a delivery, it was his problem. A corrupt cop in the 25th Precinct or a Johnny Capra laid off as much of the risk of doing business as he could on kids in the neighborhood. As the employee, an Ernie Boy would say nothing to the police about his employer if he was caught. As the employer, Capra or the corrupt cop would do as much as possible through payoffs and influence to get his boy cut loose from any entanglement with the police.

In doing business this way, the hustlers on The Avenue thought they were "collar-proof." They could never be arrested, they thought, because they themselves never participated directly in criminal transactions on the street. Their profits from The Avenue were delivered to them in safe places by their most trusted lieutenants. Capra, for instance, insisted on taking his money on a fairway of a golf course in Westchester County. Other members of the Pleasant Avenue

June 15, 1971

*The undersigned received from
Sgt. David B. Durk, sh # 266 - Personnel Bur.
one (1) Colt .38 Cal. Cobra revolver, ser #
. Revolver previously obtained from
a confidential informant*

*Capt. Ralph Romano
Intelligence Div.*

Sgt. David Durk

Where was the leak? This was the voucher signed by a captain at police headquarters for the gun the old man said he had bought through a police officer assigned to East Harlem. The old man said the same cop was also selling to drug dealers. Shortly after this Colt .38 was turned in, word reached East Harlem that headquarters was interested in the gun and the old man was told that there would be trouble if he couldn't get it back.

establishment were often paid off in Florida or in Las Vegas.

I knew that making a case against the gun-dealing cop in the 25th wouldn't be easy. He had been there for years and knew his way around.

I took the gun to police headquarters. If the gun could be traced, we might develop a lead that could eventually implicate the corrupt cop in the 25th. In the police commissioner's outer office, a captain from the Intelligence Division helped me fill out the papers that went with placing the gun in the police property clerk's office for safekeeping as evidence. And he ordered me to carve my initials and my shield number (266) on the frame of the gun, using a pair of scissors from the commissioner's office.

The FBI was contacted, and efforts were begun to trace the gun. Within hours, word somehow reached the 25th Precinct that headquarters was investigating a case involving a gun sold on The Avenue. Very few people at headquarters knew about the gun, but there clearly had been a leak.

Late that night the old man called me. He was very upset.

"David, I think they know about the gun. The girl I gave the money to is looking for it back."

I was furious. I asked the old man to tell me exactly what the girl on The Avenue said to him.

"What did she say? She said, 'Listen, what did you do with the gun?'"

"What did you say?"

"I said my cousin has it in Astoria."

"What did she say?"

"She said to get it back or I'd have trouble."

I thought for a moment. It was clear The Avenue knew there was heat downtown involving a gun, but I didn't think they knew exactly which gun. If they were really sure that the gun was the one sold to the old man, they'd be doing more than just talking to him. The strong-arm guys would already have been at his apartment.

"We've got a problem," I said, "but I think we can handle it. Just stay cool. I'll get back to you."

I called Grubert at home. We both agreed the gun had to go back, and quickly. Grubert began to lay out the procedure for getting the gun out of the property clerk's office and back to the old man. I interrupted him.

"Chief, goddamn it, I just thought of something. We've got one fucking problem. I carved my initials and my shield number on the frame of the gun. We can't give it back with my shield number on it."

Grubert had a suggestion. A gunsmith could rub out my initials and shield number with a special compound called blueing.

"Where are we going to round up a gunsmith at this hour of the night?" I asked.

Grubert said he would personally get the gun out of the property clerk's office and that somehow he would find a gunsmith to do the job. To insure the safety of the old man and to guard against any more leaks, Grubert said he would handle everything himself and would not involve any other members of the department. So, at around midnight, Assistant Chief Inspector Arthur Grubert assigned himself the legwork of rousing a gunsmith out of bed. He asked me to stand by in my apartment.

I called the old man and asked him to come over to await Grubert and the gun. We waited in the apartment and Grubert worked his way through the gunsmith fraternity in Manhattan and the Bronx. No gunsmith had the right blueing for that particular gun. Grubert wouldn't give up and said he'd look further. The old man had worked the day shift. He was yawning and beginning to nod off. By two in the morning, the old man was more tired than afraid. He said he'd like to go home and go to sleep. I told him I'd call him first thing in the morning.

Shortly after the old man left, Grubert called. He'd found a gunsmith with the right kind of blueing in Yonkers. Grubert said my initials and shield number were rubbed out and he was on the way to my apartment with the gun.

The next morning I got the gun back to the old man. He was able to show it on The Avenue, and the heat was off him. If there were headquarters cops holding a gun from The Avenue, it wasn't that gun.

The cop involved in gun dealing on The Avenue is still on the force. He was saved by the leak when we tried to trace the gun. We were never able to catch him in the act. The old man's information was not enough to bring him up on charges, and the trace itself did not tie him to the gun.

This cop and others like him are criminals who happen to wear the police uniform of the city of New York. They are particularly dangerous criminals. With the cover of legitimacy, it is all too easy for them to elude detection and arrest. And it is all too easy for them to deal in guns, drugs, and death in places like East Harlem.

15. Operation Window

In the fall of 1971, Grubert began to work in earnest on his central targets—the men who financed and ran the Pleasant Avenue heroin establishment. He moved carefully. He knew how easily a case could be blown or sold. He wanted to get "the guys who could never be gotten." He began with fourteen targets, including Capra and Inglese. Working under the tightest security, he soon expanded his target list to more than ninety names.

Grubert was deceptive. There was nothing flamboyant about him. He dressed in conservative business suits. His manner was gentle, not gruff. He rode around in a gray Plymouth. And, unlike Seedman, he shunned personal publicity. He was perhaps the least visible of the men who had real power in the police department.

The heroin dealers of Pleasant Avenue, through their connections in the Mafia family of Carmine Trumunti, had their own early-warning intelligence system. The wiseguys on The Avenue talked about their "switchboard" downtown. The switchboard was hooked into the police department, the Manhattan district attorney's office and the Justice Department in New York, Washington, and Miami. The Avenue usually knew what the cops, the Feds, and the detectives of District Attorney Hogan's office were looking into. The Trumanti organization had its own wiremen who tapped police lines and were also able to buy information from corrupt cops at headquarters.

But, in the first weeks of 1972, the mob switchboard failed. Grubert made a major move, and the switchboard didn't pick it up. Grubert's low-key approach paid off. There were no leaks out of the unit, even though it had succeeded in doing something no other unit had ever done before. Grubert had moved five undercover detectives into a second-floor apartment in a tenement on Pleasant Avenue near 118th Street.

From the apartment, the detectives had a commanding view of The Avenue. Most important, they had an unobstructed view of the Pleasant Tavern on 117th, which was the center of Zanfardino's heroin operations. They could also see the nearby barber shop where kilo and half-kilo packages of heroin were often stored awaiting delivery, and they could see the pair of public telephone booths on the northeast corner of 117th where dealers took customers' calls for shirts and pants and pillowcases.

The detectives passed themselves off as hustling gypsy cabdrivers and, somehow, for nine months everybody on The Avenue bought their act. They were never made. Nobody smelled cop, even though Grubert's detectives carried out extensive surveillance operations. Grubert had picked his men well. Although each of them worked twelve-hour tours in a roach-infested apartment for nine months in the criminal enclave of Pleasant Avenue, not one of them made a single mistake. And, during this time, by using special photographic gear* they made more than a thousand hours of

*The gear included a night camera that could take pictures in virtual darkness. The camera was equipped with an image-amplifier lens that was able to magnify available light thirty thousand times. The lens is adapted from the army's night-vision sniperscope that was developed for antiguerrilla warfare in Vietnam.

Operation Window. New York City detectives had an excellent view of heroin dealings from an apartment window near 118th Street. In this police photograph, #3 is John ("Johnny Echoes") Campopiano, #2 is Moe Lentini, #1 is not identified. (The marks were put on by the police department.) The Pleasant Tavern was the center of operations for the heroin organization run by Gennaro Zanfardino.

films and videotapes showing the major figures of the heroin establishment plying their trade.

Grubert's filmmakers made what has to be the ultimate Andy Warhol-type, *cinéma-vérité* movie on the street life of hoodlums. Thanks to the New York City Police Department, there is now in existence a thousand-hour movie, unedited, that could be titled *The Avenue.* Anyone with the patience to sit through it all would see a kind of extended Sicilian, street-corner version of *The Clockwork Orange.*

Grubert's men who sat through it making the movie are still incredulous. One detective said, "You wouldn't believe the antics of some of those guys. They got some really impressive morons with IQs of about 20 up there. Day after day, the same guys on the same street corners. And, if there wasn't any action, they went bananas. I remember a couple of times they showed up with really fancy flare guns and began shooting up flares. And I mean flares like they got on lifeboats. This is right, right in the middle of the fucking city, and they don't give a shit. You never saw a precinct sector car come near the place. Nobody bothered with those guys. They could do anything they wanted."

The detectives manning Grubert's observation post became as fascinated with their Ernie Boys as Jane Goodall did with her baboons. Like Vinnie, most of The Avenue regulars were into snorting cocaine. Their using the stuff like snuff explains much of their playfulness on the street since the cocaine made them hyper. Ernie Boy wouldn't just stand on a street corner. He'd do his thing. He'd strut, snap his fingers, do a few Cagney moves, a little Tito Puente, a little Sammy Davis, and then he'd dance by his brother-in-law Johnny Echoes Campopiano and playfully grab him by the crotch. Campopiano would bellow in mock pain and chase Ernie Boy down The Avenue and kick him in the ass. By this time, both Ernie Boy and the heftier Campopiano would be breathing heavily. They'd throw a few light punches at each other and then go back to fingersnapping and handclapping.

Ernie Boy and the others on The Avenue were high on cocaine most of the time, particularly on Sundays and Mondays when business was slow. The cocaine was used primarily as an aphrodisiac. "If you have to go to bat a lot, you got to feed the nose" was a bit of wisdom often heard on The Avenue.

The sex life of the Pleasant Avenue heroin entrepreneurs was wildly unpredictable. Nunzi might not have time for sex, but other dealers made time. Younger punks would curry

Ernie Boy's brother-in-law. Johnny Echoes (standing, in the under-shirt) on Pleasant Avenue. Campopiano picked up his nickname because he rarely said anything without repeating it at least twice. Campopiano was one of the more active and visible members of the Zanfardino heroin organization.

favor on The Avenue by bringing girls around for the pleas-ure of the older dealers. It was not unusual for an Ernie Boy to return from a trip to Jersey in the middle of the day with two or three Cuban chicks in tow. He'd bring his Caddie to a screeching stop in front of one of the storefront social clubs, jump out of the car and holler: "Showtime. All right, all you humps, here we go. Showtime."

All business would stop, and the dealers would retire to a back room for a little fun and games. These impromptu par-ties were called matinees and they might last a half hour, or they might go on until the next day.

Very few blacks were seen on The Avenue. In all the time

that Grubert's men ran what came to be called Operation Window, only two black dealers came to The Avenue to pick up heroin packages.

Gennaro Zanfardino was clearly the most visible of the street dealers on The Avenue. Zanfardino conducted business in the Pleasant Tavern and on the sidewalk outside. A customer would arrive and indicate to Zanfardino how much heroin he wanted. Zanfardino would state the price and terms of delivery. The customer would then pay cash for the heroin, up front in the Pleasant Tavern. Afterwards, he would turn over his car keys to Ernie Boy or another one of Zanfardino's delivery boys. In the usual procedure, whoever was making delivery would first go down The Avenue to the barber shop and draw a kilo or a half-kilo, whatever the customer was buying. With the heroin placed in the trunk of the customer's car, the delivery boy would drive it to some location, which might be as far away as Queens or Long Island. Then he'd make it back to the Tavern, return the car keys, and tell the customer where to find his car.

Capra, as stated earlier, didn't participate directly in any way in street sales. He was a moneyman and key figure on the smuggling side of The Avenue's business. It was believed that Capra, Herbie Sperling, and a Lebanese businessman, who was known as Murad the Arab and lived in Dobbs Ferry, New York, were the central figures in most of the heroin smuggling that went on along the East Coast in the 1960s and early 1970s. These were the guys who could sit down with the Cotronis in Montreal or the Corsican bigwigs in Paris and Marseilles and negotiate multimillion-dollar heroin deals. While Zanfardino and Inglese were strictly creatures of The Avenue, Capra and Sperling were men of the world.

16. The Trap

Early in 1972, Grubert began showing some of his video-tapes of The Avenue to Police Commissioner Patrick Murphy and other high-ranking police commanders. A few of the brass were openly contemptuous of Grubert's window-peep operation. They couldn't see the value of the tapes. "What does it prove?" one wanted to know.

"So you got guineas hanging out with guineas. Big deal. I don't see any heroin. Where's the junk? Where's the sales? Where's the evidence? Where's the cases? Why are we spending all this money taking pictures of a bunch of grease-balls when we haven't anything to show for it?"

Grubert had his critics, but Commissioner Murphy was not one of them. Murphy not only gave his full support to Operation Window but decided to try to expand the investigation by sharing Grubert's information with key federal narcotics agents assigned to major ongoing heroin investigations in this country and Europe.

Experienced federal agents didn't have to look at the tapes produced by Operation Window for very long to know what Grubert had discovered on Pleasant Avenue. Here was the nexus of heroin traffic in the United States! The Feds were able to identify several visitors to The Avenue who were unknown to Grubert's detectives. One was Enrique Barrera, a Cuban, suspected of being a major figure in an international heroin ring operating out of Belgium. Intelligence reports indicated that Barrera's so-called Belgian connection used U.S. servicemen to bring multi-kilo loads of heroin into the port of New York. The heroin was concealed in cars purchased by the servicemen in Europe and shipped to "relatives" in the States.

A federal narcotics agent, posing as a U.S. Army sergeant, had infiltrated the ring and identified Barrera as one of three distributors of heroin from the Belgian connection in the United States. Barrera's visits to Pleasant Avenue and the police tapes of his activities there were considered by the Feds to be of extreme importance.

Grubert's tapes led to the first major, long-term investigation of street traffic in heroin ever conducted in New York in which federal agents and New York City cops worked together under a joint command and with a high degree of mutual trust.

With the cops and the Feds working together in earnest, the breaks came sooner than Grubert or any of the bosses had reason to expect.

On the afternoon of February 10, 1972, the carefully concealed and insulated heroin empire of Herbie Sperling began to come apart. Louis Mileto, Sperling's neighbor in Bellmore, Long Island, and one of Herbie's most trusted underlings, was in his car driving south on the Brooklyn-Queens Expressway near La Guardia Airport. Traffic was still light; the big commuter rush would not begin for another hour.

Like Sperling, Mileto was a sharp hoodlum from Manhattan's Lower East Side who had graduated from petty street crime to the wholesale heroin business under the stern tutelage of a Mafia don, Vito Genovese.

Mileto was a man of considerable talents and fine platinum nerves. In the 1950s, he was known as one of the slickest of the jewel thieves working Manhattan's best mid-town hotels and high-society apartment buildings. In his years as a jewel thief who scored lots of ice, Mileto worked in all the best places—the Waldorf, the St. Regis, the Plaza. Working for Sperling in the heroin business, he no longer had first-class accommodations. For reasons Mileto could never figure out, Herbie felt more comfortable and secure sitting on a torn vinyl chair in the Skyline Hotel on Tenth Avenue or in one of a half-dozen third-rate motels on Long Island.

Mileto missed the vichyssoise at the St. Regis and the *pâté maison* at the Plaza, but, otherwise, he had no complaints. He no longer coveted the treasures to be found in hotel wall-safes. He had other things on his mind.

On February 10, before getting in his car to drive through Queens, Mileto had spent the morning working in a dark-ened motel room near La Guardia Airport. He'd spent hours busily mixing pure heroin with milk sugar and quinine, then weighing and packing the mixture into eighth-kilo and quar-ter-kilo bags. In the heroin business, this was Louie's special art. He worked with the confidence and dispatch of a master cake-decorator. No one in the Sperling organization could match Mileto as a mix-man. Louie could work in a room all day and not leave a trace of powder on the floor or in the drain of the bathroom sink.

Mileto was a key man in the preparation of heroin for street distribution in the United States. When a multi-kilo heroin shipment came into New York City from Sperling's London connection, Herbie's dock or airport men would bring the fresh load to Louie at the Skyline or at a Long Island motel for mixing and packaging. Louie would work the new load and, when the street packages were ready, he'd call Sperling or Sperling's chief lieutenent, Sonny Gold. A kid from The Avenue would then be sent to Louie to pick up the packages.

That's the way Sperling heroin moved week after week for years—from the boat or the airport to Louie to the kid moving street packages to the street dealers. But, on February 10, the routine was interrupted and Louie made an unusual move. Instead of calling Herbie for a kid to move that day's packages, Louie left the motel room with several eighths and quarters to make a delivery himself. This was something Louie was never supposed to do. He was a stash man and stash men stayed off the street. But, against the rules, Louie set out to drive through Queens with thirty thousand dollars' worth of heroin in his car.

About three miles south of the airport, Mileto carefully checked his rear view mirror and turned off the expressway. He drove slowly, hugging the right side of the road. If a car stayed behind him for more than two or three blocks, he pulled over and let it pass. He had no reason to expect a tail, but he was taking no chances.

Mileto drove east through the Woodside section of Queens. He looked at his wristwatch. He would be right on time.

In Rego Park, just before the overpass of the Long Island Expressway, Mileto turned into the parking lot of Wetson's Hamburger Drive-In. On the seat beside him, Mileto had a little more than a kilo of heroin in eighth-and quarter-kilo packages—all in a white shopping bag.

Slowly he drove to the back of the lot and backed his car into a parking space along the rear fence. He turned off the ignition, lit a cigarette, and waited.

It wasn't long before three men walked toward Mileto's car. Mileto knew one of the men. The other two he'd never seen before. The man Mileto knew was drinking from a paper cup. Near Mileto's car, the man put his head back and took a long swallow and as he did he eyeballed Mileto and gave him a very slight nod. Mileto returned the nod and unlocked the car doors. The man he knew slid in beside him in the front, and the other two got in the back seat.

Mileto and the others sat silently puffing on cigarettes. They looked in every direction except at each other.

Two teen-age girls carrying school books and munching hot dogs walked past the car. One of the men in the back seat broke the silence. "Look at the ass on the tall one. She ain't fifteen, if she's that, but I'll tell you that's got to be eating pussy."

Mileto laughed and turned to the man beside him. "Okay, kid, let's see it."

"Don't worry, Louie, it's all here," the young man answered. "I wouldn't drag you out to no Wetson's lot if we didn't have all the bread. The guy behind you is the heavy dude with all the bread counted out like you said. The other dude over there is his nose and his nose has got to say your stuff is okay before we turn over what we got for you. That's no problem, Louie, is it?"

Mileto took a small package of heroin out of his shopping bag and gave it to the man beside him. The man looked at it for a moment and then handed it to the man directly behind him. Louie heard somebody say, "It looks good." He heard the package being opened. Then a voice from the back. "Take your time, make sure. No hurry."

Another voice. "It's good."

"Are you sure?"

"Yeah."

Then Louie heard the man beside him scream, "What the fuck is this? You guys crazy? You shitheads trying a heist?"

Louie turned. One man was huddled over in the back seat pressed against the door with his eyes closed. The other man held a .357 magnum pistol in his hand pointed at Louie's head. "Put your hands on the dash, both of you. Don't do nothing stupid and nobody gets hurt."

Other men approached the car. It wasn't a heist. It was a visit from Uncle Sam. There were Feds all over the place. Louie and the man next to him had been drawn into a trap.

Louie's first mistake of the day was to drive to Wetson's to deliver the package. His second mistake came later when the Feds allowed him to use a telephone to call a lawyer. Instead of calling a lawyer directly, Louie called Joseph Conforti, another member of the Sperling organization. Louie told Conforti that the Feds had him, and he asked Conforti to call a lawyer. Conforti didn't call a lawyer. He called Sperling. Sperling quickly made his way to the motel room near La Guardia Airport where he knew Mileto had spent the morning working a load of heroin.

Sperling didn't know how much the Feds knew, but he took the chance of going to the motel to recover whatever heroin Mileto had left behind. In the motel room, Sperling found that Mileto was cutting the heroin into more bags than he was supposed to. Herbie saw that his old friend Louie was holding out on the organization and skimming off eighth- and quarter-kilo amounts from multi-kilo shipments. Mileto had his own action going, and this was the first Herbie knew of it.

After Sperling's visit to the motel room, Conforti did call a lawyer and Mileto was bailed out.

Several days later Mileto disappeared. At first the Feds couldn't be sure if someone had done a number on Louie or whether Mileto had simply jumped bail. Then a state trooper found a car on fire on a country road in Suffern, New York. The trooper put the fire out and in the trunk of the car he found the torso of a man's body. There were no limbs in the trunk and no head. The torso might never have been identified if a medical examiner had not found teeth inside the stomach. From dental records, the teeth were identified as Mileto's and the medical examiner theorized that Mileto had been beaten so severely that he had swallowed his own dislodged teeth during the course of the beating.

Federal agents went to see Mileto's wife, Cecile. At first, Louie's widow would say nothing. She refused to acknowledge her late husband's relationship with Herbie Sperling. But, after several months of patient questioning, Cecile Mileto broke her silence and agreed to become the government's first solid witness against Herbie Sperling and his organization.

Cecile Mileto told federal agents that her husband often took her on business trips and to meetings. She said she was present one afternoon in a lower Manhattan apartment when her husband and Herbie Sperling put together fifty thousand dollars in cash in a suitcase for use in a narcotics transaction. She remembered seeing the money and details of the conversation. This was the government's first hard information tying Sperling to a specific heroin deal, and it enabled government lawyers to get court permission to install listening devices in and around Herbie's various places of business.

On days when it wasn't raining or very cold, Herbie conducted much of his business on the corner of Seventh Avenue and Fifty-fourth Street near the Stage Delicatessen and the Ballantine barber shop. There was a mailbox on that corner and with the cooperation of postal authorities, agents put an electronic bug in the mailbox and recorded hours of Sperling's conversations.

The agents heard Sperling talk about "shirts" and "socks" and about "good niggers" and "bad niggers." They heard him talk about "action" uptown and downtown and out of town. Most days, he was in good humor, joking with his close pals, Sonny Gold and Joseph Conforti.

If Sperling worried about anything, he worried about his dealings in Europe. In 1971, the French police had raided major heroin laboratories in Marseilles and Paris. Sperling's principal heroin buyer in London was having a hard time keeping Herbie supplied. If Sperling couldn't buy heroin directly from European brokers or dealers at lab prices, he would have to buy from Capra or Nunzi or some other *goy* dealer on The Avenue and pay boat prices. In transatlantic multi-kilo heroin deals, the so-called boat price paid in New York could be double the lab price paid in London or Paris. If Herbie lost his direct European connection, his profits per kilo would go down.

More important, he would lose much of his stature in the business. Instead of being one of *the* three or four men in New York who could arrange hundred-kilo deals in Europe, he would be just another dealer, among thirty or forty, who could pick up boat packages of ten or fifteen kilos on The Avenue. He would no longer be the equal of Capra or Murad the Arab or Zanfardino. And the lawyers and businessmen from Westchester and Long Island—the moneymen who speculated in heroin deals—might not be in such a rush to hand over suitcases of cash to back Sperling drug deals.

The moneymen wanted to be in and out of heroin deals in six to eight weeks. They wanted quick return on investment. To keep his backers happy, Sperling had to be sure of a steady flow of "pure" from Europe. He didn't have time to play the nickel-and-dime games of picking up pieces of boat shipments from The Avenue. Like a Sammy Glick or a Robert Vesco or any super-promotor seeking to outdazzle other big-time hustlers, Sperling had to maintain a certain mystique. He had to be able to do and keep on doing the impossible. He had to keep the guinea kids in awe. The Vinnies and the Ernie Boys had to know what it was to work for "a Jew with real balls and with dynamite connections." The word went out from the Stage that "if a ton of the stuff ever comes in all at once, you can bet your little round ass it'll be Little Herbie's ton." And, it was more than bravado. Many people on The Avenue believed in Sperling magic. Who could out-hustle Herbie? Who had his balls? And what other Jew kid ever delivered packages for Vito Genovese when he wasn't even seventeen?

On the corner of Fifty-fourth and Seventh, Herbie Sperling was chairman of the board. He concerned himself with only the most important matters—big heroin shipments, big money deals, and the comings and goings of big customers. If a black dealer arrived from Detroit or Philadelphia to pick up five kilos he generally got a "hello" from Herbie. But, if a Spic or *shva* came down from the Bronx for a half-kilo, Herbie usually didn't have time for him. Sonny Gold or Joe Conforti handled the transaction.

Sperling gave no indication that he felt any heat from the law on his New York operations. Even after Mileto's body was found, Sperling stayed cool and did business day after day on his favorite street corner. He clearly didn't know that Cecile Mileto was ratting him out. He didn't know that hour after hour his street-corner conversations were being recorded by the bug in the mailbox, and he didn't know that agents and detectives working The Avenue had found a second witness, a young, oddball stockbroker who knew all about Sperling and the innermost secret dealings of the wholesale heroin business in New York.

This second witness, a young hustler who would eventually "bury" Sperling and twenty other major dealers on The Avenue, was thirty-one-year-old Barry Lipsky, the son of a wealthy Miami Beach hotel owner. Lipsky was a "mob groupie" who admired Sperling and all the big-action guys in narcotics. They were his idols, the most "exciting guys" he ever knew. Lipsky made a deal with the government to give up his idols only after he himself became a suspect in a brutal murder—a murder that even The Avenue couldn't cover up.

17. The Patsy Parks Murder

Like Nunzi's troublesome daughter, Stella, Barry Lipsky had little patience with the ordinary. He liked treats and parties and special occasions.

As a young boy, he liked dressing up in a ruffled shirt and a tuxedo and crashing catered affairs in the ballrooms of the Miami hotels. The son of a hotel man, young Barry had easy access to the joys of the punchbowl and the sweet table. He came to know sooner than most boys that there were better things in life than Oreo cookies and Fig Newtons. There were chestnuts Mont Blanc and strawberries cardinal and puff pastries and all kinds of goodies if you knew where to go and got there fast.

In adolescence, Barry found himself endlessly in pursuit of something better. A Porsche wasn't as good as a Maserati. The sand in Miami wasn't as white as the sand in Aruba or Martinique. Watching the Dolphins play football from an ordinary seat wasn't as good as watching from the press box. Marijuana wasn't as good as cocaine. Climbing into bed with one girl for the night wasn't as good as with two girls. And, in making money, working at a job wasn't as good as making deals.

In the late 1960s, Lipsky's dealing got him into trouble with the law. He was convicted in a stock-fraud case and placed on probation. Mafia informer Vincent Terese helped convict Lipsky by identifying him as a small-time "launderer of bad paper" for mob figures in Florida.

In April, 1971, Lipsky received permission from his probation officer to move to New York. Barry gave assurances that he would behave himself, and the transfer of his case to a probation officer in Manhattan was handled routinely.

Among criminals, Lipsky was considered to be a mouse. Any cop reviewing his record could easily conclude that Lipsky was just another stocks-and-bonds, quick-buck specialist who got his hand caught in the grimy Fort Lauderdale-Miami high-finance cookie jar.

There was nothing in Lipsky's record in 1971 to tie him to heavy criminal action, certainly not to drugs or violence. True, Vincent Terese said Lipsky knew some organized crime people. But how many stockbrokers, accountants, and lawyers in Florida didn't do business occasionally with one or two boys from the mob?

Lipsky came to New York and moved into apartment 1A at 1420 Third Avenue, corner of Eighty-first Street in Manhattan. No one in law enforcement had reason to suspect that the rent for the apartment was being paid by a Pleasant Avenue heroin dealer, Vinnie Pacelli. Nobody knew Barry Lipsky had been recruited by Pacelli to stash heroin and move packages for The Avenue. Nobody knew The Avenue considered Lipsky a perfect street operative. He had no record in New York. He didn't use heroin. He had one bullshit conviction in Florida. He wasn't Italian. And, most importantly, mob people in Miami and in the federal penitentiary in Atlanta had vouched for Barry, saying he was a "stand-up guy."

Herbie Sperling had nothing to do with bringing Lipsky into the big-time heroin business. Sperling generally didn't like to deal with strangers, but Lipsky was considered kosher by Sperling and his associates because Pacelli vouched for him.

Next to Johnny Capra, twenty-nine-year-old Vinnie Pacelli was considered to be the smartest and most sophisticated of the younger heroin dealers on The Avenue.

Pacelli had spent two years at Manhattan College. He had an honorable discharge from the Army and he was a judo and karate expert who had mastered his art in Japan. Pacelli had done something that Sperling and other dealers on The Avenue had not been able to do. Pacelli had moved the heroin business out of the ghetto. His customers were respectable, white middle-class New Yorkers.

Pacelli didn't hang out on a street corner or in dingy motels in the style of Sperling and Zanfardino. He was a leader of a new breed of hip heroin dealers who had established themselves in discothèque clubs on Manhattan's East Side and in Greenwich Village.

Pacelli's main hangout was the Hippopotamus Club on East Fifty-fourth Street. He made no secret of his mob connections and, among young people at the club, he was a source of thrills and kicks as well as of cocaine and heroin. In the disco culture of the late 1960s, Pacelli had become a cult leader. His dates told their roommates about how thrilling it was to be with a real gangster. He was actually *in* the Mafia. On the Hippopotamus dance floor girls from Lodi, New Jersey, and Windsor Locks, Connecticut, ran their fingers through Pacelli's hair and snuggled close to him. He made them laugh, and they hugged and kissed him. For his celebrity-conscious dates, going to bed with him was like going to bed with Mick Jagger or Warren Beatty or a real Black Panther.

And Pacelli was generous. He paid the rent and did favors for girls he liked. He shopped for them at Saks, at Bergdorf's, and at all the best places. For wide-eyed eighteen- and nineteen-year-old girls from the typing pools of ad and model agencies, Pacelli was indeed a celebrity and a prince.

In Vinnie Pacelli, Barry Lipsky had found his kind of guy. Pacelli's action was the ultimate turn-on, the something better Barry had been looking for all his life. Reality had surpassed imagination. It was so intoxicating—the secret dealings, the important people, the bundles of cash, the limousine rides, and the all-night parties—that Barry felt stoned all the time. He was finally on Mount Olympus with the gods!

Sadly for Barry, his reverie would not last long. A man with a badge was about to scale Pacelli's Olympus.

By May of 1971, a federal undercover agent, John Lapore, became part of the smart discotheque scene. Using the name Johnny Larro, Lapore was able to pass himself off as a young hustler looking to score large quantities of cocaine and heroin. He made a number of small drug buys from a young woman in an apartment on East Seventy-sixth Street. When he asked for a pound of heroin, the young woman said she didn't have that much and would have to make a call.

With Lapore watching her closely, the young woman made a call that would eventually lead to the downfall of The Avenue. She called a number that Lapore later was able to trace to Vinnie Pacelli.

Soon after, a pound of heroin was delivered to Lapore in the apartment on East Seventy-sixth Street. Federal agents then arrested Pacelli, the woman in the apartment, Elisa Possas, and four other people, including Pacelli's fiancée, Beverly Jalaba.

Barry Lipsky was startled by the bust, but he was not tied to the drug dealings in the apartment of East Seventy-sixth Street, and the government would not learn of his heroin activities until months later.

Incredibly, Pacelli didn't seem very upset at first by the

arrests. He and his fiancée were soon out on bail and they asked Lipsky to arrange their wedding quickly. They wanted a first-class wedding to take their minds off their troubles with the law, and that's exactly what Lipsky helped them put together.

The wedding was set for June 6, 1971. The ceremony itself was held in St. Patrick's Cathedral. In the afternoon, Barry arranged cocktails and canapés for the bridal party at the Tavern-on-the-Green Restaurant in Central Park; in the evening, he laid on a reception for two hundred people at the Pierre Hotel on Fifth Avenue.

Elisa Possas missed the wedding. She couldn't make bail. But a friend of Elisa's, Patsy Parks, a young fashion model, did attend the wedding and Johnny Larro became very interested in this young lady.

Patsy Parks also had an apartment in the building on East Seventy-sixth Street and her new friend Johnny already had information that her apartment was used by Pacelli and Elisa Possas to stash heroin. Soon, Patsy was called before a grand jury to tell what she knew. She denied having any knowledge about drug dealing, but Lapore wasn't convinced. Several months after the Pacelli wedding, another subpoena was issued for Patsy Parks to appear before a grand jury.

Patsy Parks failed to answer the government's second subpoena and, on the morning of February 4, 1972, her badly decomposed body was found in a vacant lot near a parkway in Massapequa Park, Long Island.

Working with New York City and Long Island detectives, Lapore found out that Patsy Parks had been last seen alive leaving the Hippopotamus discothèque with Barry Lipsky.

Lipsky, it was learned, had left for Miami Beach soon afterward to visit his family. Lapore contacted Lipsky's probation officer in New York. The probation officer called Barry and casually asked him to return to New York. "There's some papers here, Barry, that the office says have to be signed. I'm sorry to louse up your vacation, but you better get your ass back here."

On the evening of March 4, 1972, six New York detectives and three federal agents were waiting for Barry Lipsky at New York's La Guardia Airport. One of the agents was Bob Levinson.

"How ya doing, Barry?" Levinson asked as Lipsky stepped off a plane from Miami.

"Do I know you?" Lipsky asked.

"Now you do, pal," Levinson replied as he flashed his narcotics agent's badge.

Lipsky was taken from the airport to Mineola, to the headquarters of the Nassau County homicide squad. Lipsky sat in a chair in the middle of an interrogation room. A detective handed him enlarged photographs of Patsy Park's body as it was found in the vacant lot in Massapequa. The chief of detectives asked Lipsky if he knew Patricia Parks. Lipsky said nothing. "Listen, Barry," a detective said, "we're down to two suspects, and you're one of them. You have got five minutes to think it over."

Lipsky sat silently for a few moments looking at the pictures. Then, without further prompting, he began to talk. A stenographer was brought in, and Lipsky dictated a twenty-seven-page statement.

Lipsky said that Vinnie Pacelli had killed Patsy Parks to prevent her from testifying further before the grand jury. And Lipsky confessed that he had helped Pacelli dispose of the girl's body.

Lipsky told of going with Pacelli and Patsy Parks in Pacelli's car on a predawn ride to Long Island. Patsy Parks had come to Pacelli seeking advice on what to tell the grand jury. Pacelli told her that he would give her money and put her on a plane to South America so that she wouldn't have to testify at all. Pacelli was supposed to be driving her to Kennedy Airport. Instead, he drove past the airport out along Long Island's south shore.

Lipsky said that Pacelli had planned to kill Patsy Parks alone, without witnesses. But Lipsky said he asked to go along because "I had just never seen somebody murdered before, and I was just curious."

In Massapequa Park, Lipsky said Pacelli stopped the car and got out, saying he had to call a friend to get the cash to give Miss Parks. Pacelli disappeared for a few minutes. When he returned to the car he asked Lipsky to drive and got in the back seat next to Patsy.

Lipsky turned on the engine and started driving farther out on Long Island, away from the airport. Lipsky remembered Patsy asking Pacelli, "Where are you taking me?" And, he remembered Patsy saying to Pacelli, "Please don't do anything to me. You don't know it, but I'm a mother. I've got a seven-year-old kid in New Jersey."

Patsy screamed. Lipsky turned and said he saw Pacelli plunge a knife into Patsy Park's chest. He heard Pacelli say, "Die, you bitch," and he watched as Pacelli repeatedly stabbed the girl and then cut her throat nearly from ear to ear.

Lipsky's statement matched the medical examiner's report which said she'd been stabbed ten times.

Detectives and agents in the room could feel themselves trembling as Lipsky described the murder, but Lipsky showed no emotion. He said that Pacelli had dragged the girl's body out of the car and into the vacant lot. Then Pacelli took a gallon can of gasoline from the trunk of the car and doused the body with gasoline. Pacelli said he didn't want to light a match to set the body afire because of the gasoline on his hands. He asked Lipsky to ignite the body and Lipsky

The young don, Vincent Pacelli, Jr., and his wife, Beverly, shown here on their wedding day. Patsy Parks, a bridesmaid at the wedding, was later murdered by Pacelli to prevent her from talking to a grand jury.

Barry Lipsky under arrest.
(New York Daily News)

did. Together they watched the body burn in the early morning light.

That was Lipsky's statement.

Patsy Parks had made the mistake of trusting Vinnie Pacelli and Barry Lipsky. She never learned the difference between charm and character.

After giving his formal statement on the murder, Lipsky gave federal agents information implicating Vinnie Pacelli and Herbie Sperling and others in drug deals. And he told of his own activity in stashing heroin and in moving heroin packages for Pacelli and other dealers on The Avenue.

It began to be clear to his interrogators that Lipsky had been active in heroin because he liked the action and the risk-taking as much as the money. He was a mob buff. He wanted Lapore and Levinson to understand that all he'd been doing was trying to put a little excitement in his life. "Don't you understand, fellows, the drug scene, that's my bag."

Lipsky told federal agents that he and Pacelli took pride in their ability to "get into the pants and the closets" of nice girls like Patsy Parks—nice girls who'd "take favors and do favors."

It was in the closets of nice girls that federal agents found some of their best evidence against The Avenue. Even empty closets proved extremely valuable. Lipsky led federal agents to old "nice girl" hiding places and by carefully vacuuming the dust in these closets, the agents found traces of heroin and cocaine.

18. Operation Uncover

Pacelli was picked up by Nassau County homicide detectives. The knife used to kill Patsy Parks was found in Pelham Bay, just where Lipsky said it had been thrown. And the car in which she was killed was found by police in Wayne, New Jersey. Although burned out, the back seat still yielded bloodstains to lab technicians of the police department.

But, in a move that infuriated detectives and agents on the case, the district attorney in Nassau County, William Cahn, did not ask for a murder indictment against Pacelli. Cahn said that the only witness against Pacelli was Lipsky, an admitted co-conspirator. Cahn said that in his opinion the testimony of a co-conspirator could not bring a conviction under New York State law. So, Pacelli was indicted and, later, convicted under a federal statue for violating Miss Parks's civil rights.

The Parks case and the Pacelli arrest were all over the newspapers, but Grubert's men reported that activity on The Avenue continued as usual.

The testimony of Cecile Mileto and Barry Lipsky and conversations recorded from the bug in the mailbox on Fifty-fourth Street and other locations gave government lawyers more than they needed to indict Herbie Sperling. But there was still not enough evidence to arrest Johnny Capra and several other major targets of Operation Uncover. Grubert and the Feds decided to leave Sperling in the street until a solid case could be made against Capra and his associates.

If Sperling were to be picked up, The Avenue might quickly find out that Barry Lipsky and Cecile Mileto were prepared to testify. Knowing this, certain drug figures might panic and try to leave the country.

It was a difficult decision. No cop or Fed wanted to leave an animal like Sperling in the street. But if you picked up Sperling, you might lose Capra, Leo Guarino, and others the Feds believed they were close to getting.

Barry Lipsky was questioned by federal agents for hundreds of hours. He gave the Feds a virtual roadmap of drug activity in New York City and across the country. Several of the agents, including Lapore and Levinson, were just about the same age as Lipsky, and Lipsky came to think of them as his friends. Lipsky was a fervid fan of the Miami Dolphins and he loved to talk about football with his agent-companions during meal breaks. Miami had lost to the Dallas Cowboys in the '72 Super Bowl, but Lipsky was sure that the Dolphins would win in 1973. "With Griese, Csonka, Fernandez, and Warfield nobody is going to beat us, right, guys? Put your money on the Cowboys or some shit team like that next time, and you're going to lose."

Lipsky didn't seem to mind being in custody. He enjoyed good talk, and for him all the talk with the agents was good —it was about football and drug dealing, his two favorite topics.

At one point, several months after his arrest, Lipsky sought reassurance from Lapore. "John, you're my friend, aren't you? You're not still mad at me because of what happened to Patsy Parks?"

Lapore set Lipsky straight. "Listen, Barry. There's only one thing I want to see. I want to see Vinnie Pacelli sitting in the electric chair, and I want to see you sitting in his lap."

While the questioning of Lipsky went on, an associate of Steve ("Beansie") Della Cava of the Capra organization walked into federal narcotics headquarters in Washington and said he wanted to talk. He was given the code name "Jimmy Fats" and was put under guard in a Long Island motel, where he talked for weeks with federal agents. "Jimmy Fats" knew things about The Avenue that the old man didn't know. He knew about the East Harlem air-conditioning store that was used as a drop by Capra's people, and he had specific information on the flow of heroin from The Avenue to the Beach Rose social club in the Bronx.

Another major breakthrough came from the work of a surveillance team on The Avenue itself. One of Zanfardino's major customers, a Puerto Rican woman from the Bronx known as Dee Dee, was seen making a pickup on The Avenue and was quietly arrested several blocks away with four pounds of heroin in a shopping bag.

Dee Dee knew she faced a long prison sentence, and she agreed to cooperate in the hope of having her jail time reduced. Within range of the cameras in Grubert's window, Dee Dee made three more controlled buys of heroin from Zanfardino's street dealers.

Putting Dee Dee to work for Operation Uncover was a major coup for Grubert and the Feds. Uncover now had direct evidence against Zanfardino's top street dealers. As one agent put it, "We now had Mr. Z by the balls. He was going away, no question about it."

By November of 1972, Grubert and the Feds knew that they had enough evidence to put together airtight heroin cases against Sperling, Zanfardino, and most of the original targets of Operation Uncover. Bosses at police headquarters and in the Justice Department also knew this, and they were getting edgy. They wanted arrests, they wanted "the bastards off the street." Uncover was already one of the longest and costliest investigations of organized crime in the history of the department. But Grubert fought for more time. He didn't want to move against The Avenue without having a solid case against the key moneyman in the New York heroin business, Johnny Capra.

Capra was no less ruthless than Sperling and Pacelli and far more cautious. Grubert knew that Capra never touched heroin himself. He only handled money. And, he stayed far away from The Avenue or any other location when heroin deliveries were being made.

The only way to make a case against someone as shrewd as Capra was to get him under the federal conspiracy laws, for acting in concert with subordinates and associates who *were* moving packages and who were doing the actual street buying and selling of heroin.

Grubert waited. He waited for Capra to make a mistake. And with Christmas approaching in 1972, Capra did make a mistake. He forgot to send Dotty Ramos a Christmas present. For a man in Capra's position, it was either an oversight or an act of arrogance not to take good care of Dotty Ramos and her two small children.

Dotty Ramos's husband, Johnny, had been a loyal member of the Capra organization for years. And at Christmas time in 1972, Johnny was in the Lucas County Jail in Toledo, Ohio, facing a ten-to-twenty-year prison term. Three witnesses in Toledo had testified that Ramos was the man who had delivered five-and-a-half kilos of heroin to a railroad station drop in October, 1970. The witnesses, as it was later proved, were wrong. Ramos had not been the man. Capra knew this. And he knew that Ramos was taking the weight in the Toledo jam-up to protect another Capra associate, Joe Messina, who had actually delivered the package.

There was Johnny Ramos sitting in an Ohio jail taking the

rap for something he didn't do. No one was more loyal to
Capra and the organization. And yet it was almost Christmas,
and Johnny Capra had sent no presents to Ramos's red-brick
house on Country Club Road near the Throgs Neck Bridge in
the Bronx. Capra was violating a firmly established rule of
The Avenue. He wasn't taking care of his people. Johnny
Ramos was in the can. And Johnny Capra wasn't taking care
of Dotty and the two children.

Two of Grubert's men, Frank Jackson and Jim Nauwens,
knew Johnny Ramos well and knew how close he had been
to Johnny Capra. And they heard talk that Dotty was despon-
dent.

Cops are great players of hunches, and in November,
1972, Jackson and Nauwens played a hunch. They arranged
to have Ramos brought from Ohio to New York for a sitdown.

Both Jackson and Nauwens are excellent detectives. They
are patient men with good bladders and hard asses. They sat
for hours and listened to Ramos talk about the frame-up in
Ohio and all his troubles. They waited for the right psycho-
logical moment. They knew their man well. Both had worked
a tap on Ramos's home telephone in 1969 for hundreds of
hours.

They told Ramos that if he was truly innocent on the Ohio
charge, they would do all they could to help him. Both men
knew that Ramos had been recruited into the heroin business while still in his teens. They truly didn't consider him to
be a hopeless criminal. They believed him when he said that
he would like to be a carpenter if he could ever get out of the
drug business. They treated him gently.

Ramos knew what he was there for. He knew the detectives wanted information. He knew Jackson and Nauwens
were working Capra. He sat at the table sadly. The detectives
began to ask specific questions about the East Harlem heroin
business. They began to ask about Capra and Della Cava and

Guarino and Jermain and other suspected members of the Capra organization. They pleaded with Ramos to cooperate and to save himself. "Take a shot at another life, Johnny."

Ramos cried. He sat at a table with the two detectives sobbing quietly. Grubert's men knew how difficult it was for a young man from The Avenue to make a decision to rat out a don like Johnny Capra. They didn't rush him. Ramos smoked cigarettes and munched on sandwiches. He talked about the thirteen years he'd spent in prison on various charges since he first went to work moving packages. Crying, he said he wanted to be free to be with his family again. The detectives told him that they would try to get the government to relocate him and his family if he cooperated in making a case against Capra. They said they couldn't promise him anything but they would really do all they could. Ramos knew they meant it.

Slowly and painfully, Ramos began to talk.

The detectives learned that Stephen Beansie Della Cava was the key man in the distribution of Capra heroin. Della Cava, working out of the East Harlem air-conditioning store that Jimmy Fats had talked about, moved packages after receiving telephone instructions from Capra. Della Cava, the detectives were told, almost always made his deliveries on Sunday mornings. "He likes to work when the church bells are ringing. Not too many people are in the streets then, and it's easy to pick up a tail, if there is a tail."

Working with information provided by Ramos, Grubert moved to get court orders to tap the phone in Della Cava's air-conditioning store and at various other locations, particularly social clubs. Grubert hoped that the taps would corroborate the information coming in from Ramos and other sources.

Getting the court orders was risky business. Judges had to be told about the existence of Operation Uncover and dozens of court clerks and assistant district attorneys would be involved in processing the warrants. Veteran narcotics detectives were often court shy. Many could remember important cases being blown once cops had to tell judges and prosecutors what they were doing. The wiseguys and the mob switchboard seemed to find out quickly about requests for and the issuance of search and wiretapping warrants. Grubert and the Feds could handpick the detectives and agents working Operation Uncover, but they couldn't handpick the judges, the assistant district attorneys, the assistant U.S. attorneys, and the stenographers and clerks in New York and Washington involved in preparing the paper work for Operation Uncover warrants.

The selling of information about warrants to mobsters by corrupt court personnel was a well-known racket. But in 1971 and 1972, there was little the department could or would do about it. Making a case against a corrupt judge or a corrupt assistant district attorney or a corrupt DA squad detective was as difficult as making a case against a Capra or a Sperling. And, all too often, the judiciary was as much a criminal enclave as was The Avenue.

During the warrant issuance phase of Operation Uncover, it became clear that The Avenue *was* receiving specific information on what Uncover detectives and agents were doing.

Shortly after the placement of bugging devices in the Beach Rose and Havermeyer social clubs, heroin dealers from The Avenue stopped going to these places. And, lower-level hoodlums, who continued to frequent the clubs, joked among themselves about being on Candid Camera. The Avenue also managed to find out about a federal surveillance operation outside a suspected Capra haunt in Whitestone, Queens.

The Avenue knew the heat was on. It became a cat-and-mouse game. The major heroin dealers stayed away from locations where there were known court-ordered bugging devices, and many stopped talking at all on their home telephones. Capra wouldn't even discuss business in or near his house in New Rochelle. He and his lawyer would talk in the middle of North Avenue, a busy and wide thoroughfare several blocks away from his house.

The Avenue itself was still considered safe. At no time was there any indication that the wiseguys knew Grubert had moved a team of detectives into an apartment on The Avenue. Day after day, Ernie Boy and Johnny Echoes would be out there on the street corner as usual snapping their fingers and dancing around waiting for action. And in midtown, near the Stage Delicatessen, Herbie Sperling would be out there on the street resting his arms on the same wired mailbox.

Word reached agents of Operation Uncover that "the boys were ready. They expected a big conspiracy bust, but they weren't worried."

One agent was told that "The Avenue will take all the indictments you've got. There won't be no convictions because there won't be no witnesses."

The arrogance of The Avenue was all too clear. The wiseguys weren't running from the heat. If the government wanted to go through the trouble of drawing up indictments against them, they were ready to accept service of the papers. The dealers didn't think convictions were possible because they were sure that they could locate and kill the government's key witnesses before the cases went to trial. To be sure, one potential key witness against Capra did disappear while warrants were being issued and was presumed murdered.

The men who did the thinking for The Avenue and the Trumunti Mafia family regarded Operation Uncover as an irritant, a nuisance, not as a serious threat to their control of heroin distribution in the United States and Canada. They had been able to buy or kill their way out of trouble before, and they would do it again. The cops and the Feds could have all the arrests and headlines they wanted, but mob money and bullets would make sure there were no convictions of important people.

The Moustache Petes miscalculated. They didn't realize how much Barry Lipsky and Cecile Mileto could hurt them. They didn't know about Dee Dee or the Operation Window videotapes. And, they had not yet tested the will of men like Arthur Grubert or Deputy Police Commissioner William McCarthy.

In the wake of the Knapp Commission revelations McCarthy had been brought out of retirement by Commissioner Murphy to crack down on organized crime and corruption. Like Grubert, McCarthy was unassuming and low key. But he got the job done and he backed up his men.

When Murphy put McCarthy in command of the Narcotics Division and all units that had anything to do with organized crime, McCarthy knew little about detective work and nothing about the world of all the Funzis. But he made it his business to find out about the Funzis, the Capras, and the Sperlings—and particularly about organized crime within the police department.

McCarthy and Grubert and the Feds knew that the case against The Avenue could be easily subverted. They took every possible precaution. Witnesses were kept under heavy guard and moved from place to place and, when possible, away from the city. Unusual measures were taken to safeguard evidence such as seized kilos of heroin, the Operation Window videotapes, the dust vacuumed from Patsy Parks's closet, and every piece of paper pertaining to the case.

There were setbacks. The Avenue was able to find out about Dee Dee and the address of the hotel on Manhattan's West Side where she was being kept under guard. Mob executioners went to the hotel, but no attempt on her life was able to be made because the hit men couldn't find out what room she was in.

The most important information about Uncover—who was to be indicted, for what, and when—was kept secret until the end. Only McCarthy, Grubert, and three or four other high-ranking police and federal bosses were fully briefed.

19. Arrest of the Heroin Establishment

Early on the morning of Friday, April 13, 1973, ten sealed federal indictments were handed up in New York and New Jersey naming eighty-six individuals as co-conspirators in the Pleasant Avenue heroin establishment. Keeping secret the size of the indictments until the arrests were made was considered essential. If The Avenue knew that as many as eighty-six dealers were to be picked up at one time and that these included the top people in the organization, the wise-guys might indeed decide to run from the heat by leaving the country.

The roundup of the eighty-six was to begin shortly before midnight on the thirteenth. McCarthy had orchestrated a leak within the department—that there was to be a major operation over the weekend against drug dealers in the Chinatown district in lower Manhattan.

So, when orders went out that hundreds of detectives were to report to a special command post in midtown Manhattan that evening, it was assumed that the men would be sent into Chinatown.

Just before the detectives and federal agents were deployed, they were told the truth about the work ahead of them. Longtime members of the force were startled. As one put it, "This was no bullshit pickup . . . nothing like it ever happened before."

Herbie Sperling was arrested by cops and Feds when he stepped out of his rented Mercedes-Benz outside his home in Bellmore, Long Island. A search of the car turned up an ax under the front seat and two loaded pistols in the glove compartment. A federal agent asked Sperling what the guns were doing in the car. Sperling was indignant. "Damned if I know," he said. "And you can be fucking sure that I'll never rent no car from Avis again."

The agents also informed Sperling that his mother had been arrested at her apartment in midtown Manhattan earlier that day and was in a holding cell. Sperling shrugged his shoulders. "Listen, if you guys have a beef with her, that's her problem. Don't lay it on me. The old lady has to take her own weight."

Agents who went to Capra's house in New Rochelle were told by a startled wife he wasn't home. But, armed with a warrant, the agents were able to search the house and found Capra hiding behind his wife's pants suits in an upstairs closet.

All over the Bronx and Westchester and northern New Jersey, hoodlums were pulled out of social clubs, after-hours bars and various young women's bedrooms.

One hood was arrested as he came out of a social club at 4 A.M. carrying a shoebox. It was filled with fifty-dollar and hundred-dollar bills.

"Where are you going with that kind of money?" an agent asked.

"I was going to buy a newspaper."

The agent laughed. "Were you going to buy a paper, or a whole fucking newsstand?"

Agents and detectives making the arrests carried shotguns and some had bulletproof vests. But, through the night, there was no violence. Most of the drug dealers came along quietly with little reaction until they were all brought together in large holding cells at the federal narcotics regional headquarters building at Fifty-seventh Street and Eleventh Avenue.

In the cells, the dealers began to lose some of their cool as they began to realize that scores of people were being arrested. When Zanfardino was brought in in handcuffs, there were gasps from the hoodlums and those seated in the cells immediately stood up to show respect.

The first of the hoods to spot Capra coming down a hallway into the lockup whispered to others, "The Hook, The Hook, they fucking got The Hook."

When Sperling's mother was brought in to be finger-printed, there were jeers and shouts from the cells. "What the fuck is this? An old lady. She should be sleeping in her bed. Why you fucks bothering an old lady."

"Hey, you guys in there shut up. You hear me? Shut up." It wasn't an agent talking. It was somebody in an adjoining cell.

There was a shout back. "Yeah, who says so?"

"This is The Hook, you pricks. The Hook. Knock it off."

There was immediate silence. The jeering was over for the night. One by one, the wiseguys were called from their cells to be fingerprinted and photographed. By dawn, sixty-five of the eighty-six named in the indictments were in custody.

Anthony Pohl, who directed the roundup for the Feds, called it "an historic night."

Commissioner McCarthy said: "Nothing has ever been done before that will so diminish the supply of drugs on the streets of New York City."

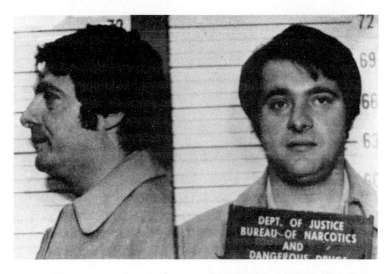

Herbie Sperling. Once a delivery boy for Mafia chieftain Vito Genovese, "Little Herbie" was driving a Mercedes-Benz when he was picked up by Operation Uncover agents near his plush home on Long Island. Agents found two loaded pistols and an ax in Sperling's car.

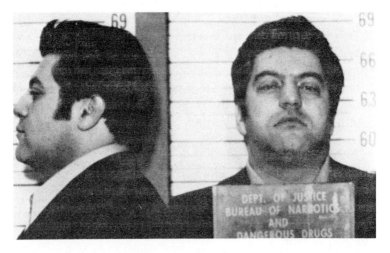

Johnny (The Hook) Capra. When federal agents arrested Capra at his home in New Rochelle, New York, they found him in an upstairs closet. One of Capra's closest associates, Johnny Ramos, testified against Capra in federal court. The Hook's mistake: he had failed to send Ramos's wife a Christmas present when Ramos was in prison in Ohio.

The fall of Jerry Z. One of the major targets of Operation Uncover, Jerry Zanfardino, shortly after his arrest in April 1973. (Don Hogan Charles, *New York Times Pictures*)

Mother Sperling. Federal agent Robert Levinson escorts Herbie Sperling's mother, Cecile, to her arraignment on drug charges. She was acquitted. (Don Hogan Charles, *New York Times Pictures*)

20. The Old Man Celebrates

The old man called me when he heard about the mass arrests, and we arranged to meet on a dock on the Jersey side of the Hudson.

"What can I tell you, David? I'm so proud and I'm so afraid. I've read every newspaper. I even read the Italian paper. I'd read the Jewish paper, too, if I could read it. Can you imagine an old greaseball like me sitting in the subway reading a Jewish paper? Mother of Mary, what a day! What a thing to happen!

"Maybe you did it, David. Maybe you took the devil out of Harlem. Maybe there won't be nothing to put in the needle no more."

The old man offered me a cigar. "I never seen you smoke one of these, but today is a special occasion."

The old man gave me a Corona Corona from a five-pack.

"I see, David, they're holding Zanfardino in a quarter of a million dollars' bail. You know I didn't know his name was Zanfardino. Jerry Z., I knew. Jerraz, I knew. But I see this guy every day for years, I never knew he has a name Zanfardino.

"And, Ernie Boy? The papers call him Oreste. Oreste Abbamonte. Where did they get Oreste from? His mother don't call him Oreste.

"And, they got him in $ 100,000 bail. The fucking punk. He probably thinks he's a big shot with a bail like that. Cash bail,

I think. The shitheel ain't no wiseguy no more. A federal rap he's got. That ain't no spitting on the sidewalk. He better say bye-bye to the house in Sands Point and to the Thunderbird he's got and to the suede vests and the fancy shoes. Everything is bye-bye. The cunt he's got will be swinging a bag on Eighth Avenue to get him candy money. He's got a big, big headache, and three Jewish lawyers wouldn't do him no good now."

The old man lit up the stub of his cigar and looked out across the water. "People on The Avenue don't believe it. I was over to Angelo's house, and everybody is talking about you and the old man that told you everything that's doing on The Avenue. Angelo's sister-in-law, the one that had the thyroid operation, she's so glad that Ernie Boy is locked up. She says if she knew who the old man was, she'd kiss him. Can you imagine that? I'm sitting right there, and that's what she says. She says she could kiss him. She's talking about me and she don't even know it.

"But, I'll tell you, David, it's not going to be so good for me. Angelo's cousin heard already that Nunzi is putting up fifty thousand dollars to find the old man. There's fifty thousand in the street to kill me, to find out who I am. You don't think Joe Pelham Bays and every punk from 116th Street isn't looking to make that fifty grand?"

The old man was truly scared, and I asked him if there was anything I could do.

"You can't do nothing. I just stay put. I go down in the morning like always and buy cigarettes in Nunzi's place and talk to people I know like always. I play dominoes with Angelo, and nobody knows from nothing."

"Maybe it's time you should move away," I said.

"Moving away right now would be the worst thing I could do. I've got to stay put. It wouldn't look right and, anyway, how could I tell Evelina out of the blue that we should move

Told City About Drug HQ in '69

By CARL J. PELLECK

The "command post" for major narcotics dealers rounded up last weekend was first pinpointed by Knapp Commission witness Sgt. David Durk in January, 1969, but was reportedly ignored by high police officials and mayoral aide Jay Kriegel for more than two years.

The roundup of most of the 86 persons named in federal indictments was termed the "largest crackdown in history" Monday, when officials said many of those indicted included "the biggest dealers in the city — people we thought we could never touch."

Nobody bothered to mention that Durk was the man who for months in 1969 tried to expose the narcotics hub with no success.

An Acknowledgement

Yesterday, First Deputy Police Commissioner William H. T. Smith acknowledged that Durk had provided the original information to police that Pleasant Av. near 116th St., in East Harlem was a major focal point for the metropolitan area narcotics underworld.

Smith said that Durk's information had apparently fallen on deaf ears until sometime after Police Commissioner Murphy took over in October, 1970. Smith said

that because of Durk's cooperation with the Knapp Commission, Murphy had ordered a full review of all charges made by the young cop.

In June, 1971, former Asst. Chief Inspector Arthur Grubert, in charge of the Intelligence Division, interviewed Durk and ordered a full investigation.

In an account of Durk's experiences published May 31, 1971, he said he first learned of the narcotics operation from "an old Italian who decided to talk to me because he was afraid his son might become a $3500 a week courier."

He said the old man told him how the narcotics were distributed, where much of it was stored and provided names and addresses of many dealers.

Gambling Element

"The most significant thing about this information," Durk said," was that it indicated a number of major Italian gamblers were deeply involved" in pushing heroin. "At that time the Mafia was believed to be out of narcotics."

It was learned that during that time Durk made numerous trips to he Pleasant Av. area, sometimes with the old man with him, and had taken down license numbers of people doing business with the drug merchants.

At that time the Special Investigation Unit of the Police Narcotics Division reportedly said they could not find any cars in the area belonging to mob figures. Most of Durk's investigating was done when he was off-duty while he was assigned as a detective on the staff of former City Investigation Commissioner Robert Ruskin.

Durk said he gave his information to Ruskin, who passed it on to former Police Commissioner Leary.

When nothing came of it by March, Durk told Kriegel, whom he had befriended during the first Lindsay campaign. He also took Kriegel to Pleasant Av. and showed him the mob's layout.

Payoff Charges

At Knapp Commission hearings, Durk testified that Kriegel had told him then that nothing could be done about Durk's charges that the narcotics mob was operating by paying off cops. Durk said that Kriegel's excuse was that an election was forthcoming.

Kriegel later denied the statement.

"The allegation that I would have said we couldn't investigate a narcotics case because of an election, a primary, is to me outrageous and is incredible and certainly is not the facts," Kriegel told the Knapp panel.

Smith said that after Grubert established that Durk's story was solid, the police Organized Crime Unit got into the investigation. When they realized how widespread the operation was, the Joint Narcotics Task Force, which includes city, state and federal agents, was brought into the investigation.

Although 250 agents were involved in last weekend's raids, Durk, a member of the Organized Crime Unit, wasn't told about it.

from The Avenue? Why? What could I tell her? The apartment's not big enough no more? All there is, is the two of us. And, she got her sister Sophie here and I got Angelo. What have we got to go someplace and start fresh again? There's no kids no more in my house, in Angelo's house. . . ."

Suddenly, the old man choked up. He must have thought of Angelo's dead son or his own son, Vinnie.

A flock of seagulls circled overhead, and one landed on a wooden post about three feet from us.

"In the sky, it don't look like such a big bird, does it, David? It's not an eagle, but it's not a pigeon."

The old man looked at the gull for a long time. More than once, he told me that it was bigger than a pigeon. After a while we walked off the pier, he told me to be careful, and he walked on to his car and left.

Four years before, the old man had come to me in his struggle to be a father for his son, a son he could no longer get himself to talk about. It wasn't easy to be a father on Pleasant Avenue, not for the old man or for Angelo or for any of the men who played dominoes together and who wanted their sons to be something more than hustlers or addicts.

On Pleasant Avenue, only a deeply troubled man would have dared talk to a cop about the heroin business. That was true in 1969, and it is true now. The old man did talk to me, he talked to Nunzi in one kind of sitdown and to Grubert in another, and he stood up for all of us. He had the courage that is born of fear—the courage that comes to fathers when they become afraid for their children.

I had failed the old man. The department had failed him. It took too long to lock up Ernie Boy. The old man wanted action taken when Ernie Boy was nineteen and when his son was eighteen. Nothing happened until Ernie Boy was twenty-

Story of the arrest. (*The New York Post,* April 18, 1973.)

three and Vinnie was twenty-two. If Ernie Boy had been locked up when the old man had wanted him locked up, it might have been different for Vinnie. I don't know. By the time I got somebody to listen to me in the police department it was too late for Vinnie and countless other kids who went the way of the needle or the fast buck.

As best I know, Vinnie is still out on the street, hustling. And, there are plenty of hustles out there for a sharp kid. There are plenty of criminal employers like Nunzi and Jewish Sam to hook up with. And, on those rare occasions, when heat comes to one racket, there's always another racket to get into. When the FBI finally cracked down hard on the FHA rackets, Jewish Sam went into brokering illegal alien deals. Vinnie fooled around with hijacking and dealing in swag. And, one of Vinnie's friends got himself a fancy job with a recording company buying drugs on the road for rock performers.

Sadly, much of the industry that is now left in New York City is criminal industry. There is the marketing of counterfeit stocks and bonds or phony lottery tickets or drivers' licenses or Green Stamps, you name it. There are the mob labs turning out LSD powder, methamphetamine, bennies, ups and downs, marijuana additives, and all the other junk they peddle on the streets and on the college campuses. There's the gun traffic. There's the booming business of stripping and selling engines and other parts from stolen cars. There are all the get-rich schemes at the airports for the customs guys and the hustlers and the freight handlers. There's arranged arson and insurance fraud. There are all the rip-offs of the city in phony methadone and Medicaid programs. And, for the untalented hood or the beginner, there is always street crime—mugging, knifing kids in Central Park for their bicycles, that sort of thing. There are so many Vinnies and Ernie Boys and worse, and so little is done with them when they are caught, that it is easy to understand why good cops become cynical. Cynicism can be self-medication for those who feel sick from frustration.

As they say, modesty is not a flower that grows in my garden. I am damned proud of April 13, 1973, and the fall of the Pleasant Avenue heroin fiefdom. We hurt the bastards real good. I would have liked to have been in the street with Bob Levinson and John Lapore when it all happened, not on the sidelines. I was on the sidelines because I was still *persona non grata* to many bosses in the department. SIU had a piece of Operation Uncover, and there were still some of the old guys around who wouldn't have worked well with Durk. But the department did put out the story of the old man and me and how Operation Uncover got started, and Commissioner McCarthy gave me command of an important undercover operation against organized crime in the garment center. For more than a year and a half, in the company of fine men and women on the force, I did get the chance to be directly involved in taking the hustlers off the street in the garment area—but that's another story.

21. The New Heroin Establishment

After April 13, 1973, the Italians on Pleasant Avenue lost much of their control over heroin distribution in the United States. But, except for a momentary disruption, the flow of heroin into this country was not slowed. The Moustache Petes who had run the business for years were out of action, but their action was taken over by new, more aggressive criminal entrepreneurs.

In Harlem, in Detroit, in Toledo, in Miami, in Watts there is now a new big-time heroin establishment made up of blacks, Chicanos, Cubans, and Chinese.

The Ernie Boys and the Vinnies were right. The old Moustache Petes didn't know how to run the business. They were too cautious. They didn't know how to make maximum profits from junk. The major black dealers now controlling the business, men like Frank Mathews, put the old Moustache Petes to shame. Mathews controls his heroin from the lab down to the $10 bag sold on the street corner. Profit on investment is more than fiftyfold. The heroin business has never been better. There is vast new opium poppy cultivation in Mexico, Burma, and Cambodia. Heroin is now being sold in many places in this country as casually as marijuana. And there is little public demand or support for truly effective narcotics law enforcement.

With blacks running the business, rather openly, in

densely populated, troubled ghettos, police bosses often decide not to make an arrest of a heroin dealer rather than risk
the possibility of setting off a street disturbance. Few police
hesitate about going into a busy bar on Eighth Avenue in
Harlem to get a man with a gun but, all too often, many now
have second thoughts about going in to pick up a man with
a half-kilo of heroin. Narcotics detectives and their superiors
have become uncertain of themselves and uncertain of public support. Black dealers have exploited this uncertainty.
The ghetto has become their sanctuary, and they have pros-
pered. Men who were once victims of oppression have become oppressors themselves. And the lion's share of the
profits from the addiction of black children is now going to
blacks.

If anything can be said for the heroin business, it is that it
has become an equal opportunity employer. And, multi-kilo
black dealers like Frank Mathews, Black Zack Robinson,
Nicky Barnes, Rufus Boyd, and Spanish Raymond owe a
great debt to punks like Ernie Boy and Vinnie Pacelli who
once brought them their first packages from The Avenue.

The Moustache Petes wouldn't have much to do with the
black street dealers. But their sons and nephews—their delivery boys—came to admire certain blacks, and this admira-
tion led to the breaking of the color line in the multi-kilo
heroin business.

A federal informant remembers the first time he met Black
Zack. Ernie Boy brought Zack to the Sutton Place apartment
of a white call girl to get him laid. The girl demurred. "I ain't
balling with no nigger," she told Ernie Boy.

"Listen, you bitch," Ernie Boy shot back, "Zack is my man,
I don't care if he's a nigger—or a zebra—you're doing him."

The girl did as she was told. And Black Zack and many of
Ernie Boy's uptown customers came to know the favors of
that Sutton Place apartment as they worked themselves up

in the heroin business and in the Harlem power structure.

Heroin was the road up for the Moustache Petes of Pleasant Avenue. It was the road up for their sons and nephews. And now it is the road up for the new *black* Moustache Petes of the 1970s.

Heroin has been a hustler's dream. There is no faster buck to be made, but the price of all these profits is measured in the lives of our sons and daughters.

A final word on SIU. There were sixty detectives in the outfit when I went to see Captain Tange with the old man's information in 1969. Forty-three of these detectives are now under indictment or in jail for narcotics corruption or for other crimes. Two used their service revolvers to end their lives when they knew they faced prosecution. One detective sergeant drank himself to death. And Captain Tange made a deal. He was given immunity from prosecution in return for testifying against the men in his command.

And, on Sundays, the old man sits on a folding chair on The Avenue playing dominoes with Angelo while both watch other men's children go up the street to Holy Rosary for communion.

Epilogue: Where They Are Now

Oreste (Ernie Boy) Abbamonte is serving an eight-year sentence in the federal penitentiary at Atlanta, Georgia.

Among his fellow inmates are: Herbie Sperling, serving a life sentence; Vinnie Pacelli, also serving life; Gennaro Zanfardino and Louis (Gigi) Inglese, serving forty years; John (Johnny Echoes) Campopiano, serving twenty years; and Johnny Capra, Stephen Della Cava, Leo Guarino, and Thomas (Moe) Lentini, each serving twelve years.

Nunzi is free after serving a jail sentence of less than four years.

Armando was not arrested and is still a dominant figure on The Avenue.

Cecile Sperling, Herbie's mother, was tried and acquitted of all charges.

Johnny Ramos, after testifying against Johnny Capra, was relocated by the federal government and is now living with his family under a new identity.

Barry Lipsky is in protective custody and is a government witness in cases still pending against suspected heroin dealers.

The old man is dead.

1976

Appendix: Knapp Commission Statement

This is the statement David Durk delivered before the Knapp Commission. It reveals why he fought the fight he did in his unsuccessful five-year effort to get either his superiors or New York City to do something about police corruption.

At the very beginning, the most important fact to understand is that I had and have no special knowledge of police corruption. We [police officers] just knew these things because we were involved in law enforcement in New York City and any experienced officer who says he didn't know had to be blind, either by choice or incompetence. The facts have been there waiting to be exposed.

This commission, to its enormous credit, has exposed them in a period of six months. We simply cannot believe, as we do not believe today, that those with authority and responsibility in the area, whether the district attorneys, the police commanders, or those in power in city hall, couldn't also have exposed them in six months, or at least in six years —that is, if they had wanted to do it.

Let me be explicit. I'm not saying that all those who ignored the corruption were themselves corrupt. Whether or not they were is almost immaterial in any case. The fact is that the corruption was ignored.

These are very tough things to believe if you're a real cop

because being a cop means believing in the rule of law. It means believing in a system of government that makes fair and just rules and then enforces them.

Being a cop also means serving, helping others. If it's not too corny, to be a cop is to help an old lady walk the street safely, to help a twelve-year-old girl reach her next birthday without being gang-raped, to help the storekeeper make a living without keeping a shotgun under his cash register, to help a boy grow up without needles in his arm.

And, therefore, to me, being a cop is not just a job but a way to live a life. Some people say that cops live with the worst side of humanity, in the middle of all the lying and cheating, the violence, and hate. And I suppose, in some sense, that's true.

But being a cop also means being engaged with life. It means that our concern for others is not abstract, that we don't just write a letter to the *Times* or give $10 to the United Fund once a year.

It means that we put something on the line from the moment we hit the street every morning of every day of our lives. In this sense, police corruption is not about money at all. Because there is no amount of money that you can pay a cop to risk his life 365 days a year. Being a cop is a vocation, or it is nothing at all.

And that's what I saw being destroyed by the corruption in the New York City Police Department, destroyed for me and for thousands of others like me.

We wanted to believe in the rule of law. We wanted to believe in a system of responsibility. But those in high places everywhere, in the police department, in the D.A.'s office, in City Hall, were determined not to enforce the law and they turned their heads when law and justice were being sold on every street corner.

We wanted to serve others, but the department had become a home for drug dealers and thieves. The force that was supposed to be protecting people was selling poison to their children. And there could be no life, no real life for me, or anyone else on the force, when, every day, we had to face the facts of our own terrible corruption.

I saw that happening to men all around me, men who could have been good officers, men of decent impulse, men of ideals, but men who were without decent leadership, men who were told in a hundred ways every day to go along, forget the law, don't make waves, and shut up.

So they did shut up. They did go along. They did learn the unwritten code of the department. They went along, and they lost something very precious—they weren't cops anymore. They were a long way toward not being men anymore.

And all the time I saw the other victims, too, especially the children, children of fourteen, fifteen, and sixteen, wasted by heroin, turned into street-corner thugs and whores, ready to mug their own mother for the price of a fix.

That was the price of going along. The real price of police corruption, not free meals or broken regulations, but broken dreams and dying neighborhoods and a whole generation of children being lost.

That was what I joined the department to stop, so that was why I went to the *New York Times,* because attention had to be paid, in our last desperate hope that, once the facts were known, someone must respond.

Now it's up to you.

I speak to you now as nothing more and nothing less than a cop, a cop who's lived on this force and who's staying on this force and therefore is a cop who needs your help.

I and my fellow policemen, we didn't appoint you, and you don't report to us. But all the same, there are some things as policemen we must have from you.

First, we need you to fix responsibility for the rot that was allowed to fester. It must be fixed both inside and outside the department.

Inside the department, responsibility has to be fixed against those top commanders who allowed or helped the situation to develop. Responsibility has to be fixed because no patrolman will believe that he should care about corruption if his superiors can get away with not caring.

Responsibility also has to be fixed because commanders themselves have to be told again and again, and not only by the police commissioner, that the entire state of the department is up to them.

And, most of all, responsibility has to be fixed because it's the first step toward recovering our simple but necessary conviction that right will be rewarded and wrongdoing punished.

Responsibility must also be fixed outside the police department, on all the men and agencies that have helped bring us to our present pass, against all those who could have exposed this corruption but never did.

Like it or not, the policeman is convinced that he lives and works in the middle of a corrupt society—everyone else is getting theirs, why shouldn't he? If anyone really cared about corruption, why wasn't something done about it a long time ago?

We are not animals. We're not stupid, and we know very well, we policemen, that corruption does not begin with a few patrolmen. And that responsibility for corruption does not end with one aide to the mayor or one investigations commissioner. . . . We know that there are many people beyond the police department who share in the corruption and its rewards.

So your report has to tell us about the district attorneys, the courts, and the bar, about the mayor and the governor—what they have done or failed to do, and how great a measure of responsibility they also bear.

Otherwise, if you suggest, or allow others to suggest, that the responsibility belongs only to the police, then for patrolmen on the beat and in the radio cars, this commission will be just another part of the swindle.

This is a harsh statement, an impolite and a brutal statement, but it's also a statement of the truth.

Second, you have to speak to the conscience of this city. Speak for all of those without a voice, all those who are not here to be heard today, although they know the price of police corruption more intimately than anyone here.

The people of the ghetto and all the other victims, those broken in mind and spirit and hope, perhaps more than any other people in this city, they depend upon the police and the law to protect not just their pocketbooks, but their very lives and the lives and welfare of their children.

Tow-truck operators can write off bribes on their income tax. The expense-account executive can afford a prostitute. But no one can pay a mother for the pain of seeing her children hooked on heroin.

This commission, for what I am sure are good reasons, has not invited testimony from the communities of suffering of New York City, but this commission must remind the force, as it must tell the rest of the city, that there are human lives at stake, that when the police protect the narcotics traffic, they and we are participating in the destruction of a generation of children.

It is this terrible crime for which you are fixing the responsibility, and it is this terrible crime against which you must speak with the full outrage of the community's conscience.

Third, as a corollary, you must help to give us a sense of priorities, to remind us that corruption, like sin, has its gradations and classifications.

Of course, all corruption is bad, but we cannot fall into the trap of pretending that all corruption is equally bad. There is a difference between accepting free meals and selling narcotics. And, if we are unable to make that distinction, then we are saying to the police that the life of a child in the South Bronx is of the same moral value as a cup of coffee. And that cannot be true for this society, or for its police force. So you must show us the difference.

Finally, in your deliberations, you must ask the policemen of this city for the best that is in them, for what most of them wanted to be, for what most of them will be. If we try.

Once, I arrested a landlord's agent . . . who offered to pay me if I would lock up a tenant who was organizing other tenants in the building. As I put the cuffs on the agent and led him away, a crowd of people gathered around and actually shouted, *"Viva la policia!"*

Of course it was not just me, or even the police that they were cheering, they were cheering because they had glimpsed, in that one arrest, the possibility of a system of justice that could work to protect them, too.

They were cheering because if that agent could be arrested, then that meant that they had rights, that they were citizens, that maybe one day life would be different for their children.

For me, that moment is what police work is all about. But there have been far too few moments like that, and far too many times when I looked into the faces of the city and saw not hope and trust but resentment and hate and fear.

Far too many of my fellow officers have seen only hate. Far too many of them have seen their dreams of service and justice frustrated and abandoned by a corrupt system—superiors and politicians who just don't care enough.

It has taken Frank Serpico five years of his life as it's taken me five years of mine to help bring this commission about.

It has taken the lives and dedication of thousands of others to preserve as much of a police force as we have.

It has taken many months of effort by all of you to help show this city the truth.

What I ask of you now is to help make us clean again, to help give us some leadership we can look to, to make it possible for all the men on the force to walk at ease with their better nature and with their fellow citizens and, perhaps one day, on a long summer night, hear again the shout, *"Viva la policia!"*

Amherst College Citation

In 1972, David Durk received an honorary doctorate of laws degree from Amherst College, with the following citation:

Dectective Sergeant of the New York City Police Department, your College greets you with the proudest title of all, "A Good Cop." At a time in history when for too many "law and order" has become a code word for repression, you have had the courage and the tenacity to challenge the conscience of every citizen, to combat the cynicism which threatens to corrode our confidence, and to insist that the only road to order is through the proper administration of justice. Your responsibility in your own life to the demands of your professional calling sets us all a high standard. If we cannot make the institutions of our society work to serve their ideal ends, then the end will be, in your own words, "broken dreams . . . and a whole generation . . . lost." Your College is especially in your debt because you expand our imaginations of what a man educated here might do to achieve a more decent and a more humane society. For that we honor you.

Acknowledgments, *Ira Silverman*

Even in grim undertakings, nice things do happen to you. Virginia Hilu happened to me. A fine editor, Virginia got this book started and saw to it that it reached publication. She brightened many dark days with good sense and good humor.

For some special insights into the operation of criminal industries in New York City, I am grateful to three colleagues: Aaron Fears, Tom Kane, and John Fitzpatrick.

I. S.